Hispanic–Latino Entrepreneurship

Hispanic–Latino Entrepreneurship

Viewpoints of Practitioners

J. Mark Munoz and
Michelle Ingram Spain

BEP BUSINESS EXPERT PRESS

Hispanic–Latino Entrepreneurship: Viewpoints of Practitioners
Copyright © Business Expert Press, LLC, 2015.

First published in 2015 by
Business Expert Press, LLC
222 East 46th Street, New York, NY 10017
www.businessexpertpress.com

ISBN-13: 978-1-60649-356-4 (paperback)
ISBN-13: 978-1-60649-357-1 (e-book)

Business Expert Press Entrepreneurship and Small Business Management
Collection

Collection ISSN: 1946-5653 (print)
Collection ISSN: 1946-5661 (electronic)

Cover and interior design by Exeter Premedia Services Private Ltd., Chennai, India

First edition: 2015

10 9 8 7 6 5 4 3 2 1

Printed in the United States of America.

Abstract

The Hispanic–Latino community is large, expanding, and an important contributor to the U.S. economy. Numbering over 50 million, they currently represent about 16 percent of the population. This number is estimated to rise to about 102 million by 2050. Hispanic Latinos engage in a diversity of jobs that help keep the American economic engine running. The practice of entrepreneurship has been on the rise with over 2.3 million businesses in the United States categorized as Hispanic owned, generating over $345 billion in sales.

This book examines the entrepreneurial mindset of Hispanic–Latinos in the United States. With limited literature on the subject, the authors created a pioneering book that captures the viewpoints of real-life Hispanic–Latino entrepreneurs. Using a 15-item questionnaire, the authors obtained information on entrepreneurial intent, goals, and business strategies utilized. Among several findings, the completed study uncovered that (1) real world experiences and challenges are relevant frameworks for entrepreneurial success, (2) race has not posed as a barrier for entrepreneurial pursuit, and (3) hardwork, discipline and a positive mindset are anchors for success. The literature offers inspirational stories and innovative ideas that define a new age of business in the United States. The book is valuable to the Hispanic–Latino community, teachers and students of entrepreneurship, executives and entrepreneurs, government officials and organizations, policy makers, and minority entrepreneurs worldwide.

Keywords

entrepreneurship, hispanic entrepreneurship, latino entrepreneurship, ethnic entrepreneurship, immigrant entrepreneurs, transnational entrepreneurs

Contents

CHAPTER 1

Introduction

America is a melting pot of entrepreneurs from around the world. It has long been known as the land of milk and honey. It is a haven where ordinary men and women possessing a dream and the desire to work hard can achieve wealth and prosperity.

There are in fact many that have found prosperity in America. The number of U.S. households worth at least $1 million rose to 9.6 million in 2013 (Fox 2014).

Many millionaires in America have amassed their fortune by starting a business or engaging in the practice of entrepreneurship.

In this book, entrepreneurship is defined as a person engaged in the process of gathering resources to create and build a business enterprise by leveraging creativity, risk, and innovation (Harwood 1982).

Entrepreneurs in America come from diverse backgrounds. Some are well educated, others are not. Some are born in the country, others are immigrants. There is a wide breadth of cultural practices, beliefs, and modalities of business.

This book brings into focus the entrepreneurial thinking of an important segment of the American economy—the Hispanic–Latino entrepreneur.

There is a distinction in the terms Hispanic and Latino. In this book, the authors combine the terms for convenience and to encompass a broader population segment. Combining the terms expands research sources on the topic. The authors mention terms separately when the research data gathered specifically mentions one group and not the other.

The term Hispanic does not necessarily refer to race, rather it defines a region of origin. It refers to individuals whose origins are Mexican, Puerto Rican, Cuban, Central or South American, or other locations that were under Spanish colonial rule. The term Latino (gender neutral) refers to individuals whose origins are countries or cultures once under the Roman rule such as Italy, France, Spain, and Brazil (Wolfe 2012).

There are other interpretations behind the Hispanic and Latino terminologies. The U.S. Census (2010) defines Hispanic or Latino as "a person of Cuban, Mexican, Puerto Rican, South or Central American, or other Spanish culture or origin regardless of race." Stone et al. (2006, 9) defined *Hispanic* as "the group of residents of the United States who trace their ancestry or origins to the Spanish-speaking regions of Latin America and the Caribbean."

Studies suggest that most of those of Hispanic or Latino origin find either label as acceptable. In one Hispanic–Latino research study, it was found that: (1) 51 percent claimed they have no preference on the term Hispanic or Latino, and (2) among those who expressed a preference, *Hispanic* is preferred over *Latino* (Taylor et al. 2012). A 2013 Gallup study found that 70 percent of Hispanics claimed that it does not matter to them whether they are labeled *Hispanic* or *Latino* (Jones 2013).

Limited studies have been made on Hispanic–Latino entrepreneurship (Shim and Eastlick 1998). There is a need for a deeper exploration into the business mindset and motivation of this important sector in the United States.

Past studies and research on Hispanic–Latino entrepreneurship point out to an important and rapidly expanding ethnic group with a motivated psyche, limited by background-related social situations, but uniquely poised for an opportunity toward betterment.

Environment

The Hispanic–Latino community constitutes a significant portion of the United States. Since 2010, the number of Hispanics in the United States exceeded 50 million making them the largest minority group in the country, consisting of approximately 16 percent of the population (Porter 2011; A.C. Nielsen 2013). About two-thirds (64.6 percent) or 33.5 million are of Mexican origin (Pew Research 2013). The Hispanic population is projected to reach 102 million by 2050 (U.S. Census Bureau 2006). Hispanic women, known as Latinas, are estimated to constitute about 30 percent of the U.S. female population by 2060 (A.C. Nielsen 2013).

The Hispanic population comprise of people from different national origins. The 14 largest Hispanic groups are as follows: Mexicans (33,539,000), Puerto Ricans (4,916,000), Salvadorans (1,952,000), Cubans (1,889,000), Dominicans (1,528,000), Guatemalans (1,216,000), Colombians (989,000), Spaniards (707,000), Hondurans (702,000), Ecuadorians (645,000), Peruvians (556,000), Nicaraguans (395,000), Venezuelans (259,000), and Argentineans (242,000) (Pew Research 2013).

The states with the highest Hispanic population in 2012 were: California (14.5 million), Texas (10 million), Florida (4.5 million), New York (3.6 million), and Illinois (2.1 million) (Krogstad and Lopez 2014).

The growth of the Hispanic population differs across the states. The states with the fastest growing Hispanic population from 2000 to 2012 were: Tennessee (163 percent), South Carolina (161 percent), Alabama (157 percent), Kentucky (135 percent), and South Dakota (132 percent) (Krogstad and Lopez 2014).

Approximately 75 percent of Hispanics are U.S. citizens, with higher number of cases among Puerto Ricans, Spaniards, Cubans, Mexicans, and Nicaraguans (Pew Research 2013).

The median household income of Hispanics is $39,000. The median income for the various Hispanic groups is as follows: Argentineans ($55,000), Spaniards ($53,000), Peruvians ($50,000), Venezuelans ($50,000), Ecuadorians ($48,600), Colombians ($48,000), Nicaraguans ($46,700), Salvadorans ($40,000), Cubans ($38,600), Mexicans ($38,000), Guatemalans ($36,400), Puerto Ricans ($36,000), Dominicans ($32,300), and Hondurans ($31,000) (Pew Research 2013).

Other relevant characteristics of Hispanics are: (1) about 36 percent of Hispanics are foreign born, with higher incidences among Venezuelans, Peruvians, Colombians, Guatemalans, and Hondurans; (2) approximately 66 percent of Hispanics are English proficient, with higher incidences among Spaniards, Puerto Ricans, Argentineans, Venezuelans, and Mexicans; (3) about 13 percent of Hispanics have a bachelor's degree or higher, with most number of cases among Venezuelans, Argentineans, Spaniards, Colombians, and Peruvians; and (4) about 55 percent of U.S. Hispanics belong to the Roman Catholic Church (Pew Research 2013, 2014).

There are unique cultural attributes of Hispanics and Latinos. For instance, compared to the general public, Latinos tend to hold more conservative viewpoints on social issues, but more liberal views in politics (Taylor et al. 2012). Hispanic culture tends to be traditional, have high regard for authority, and one that steers away from risk and uncertainty (Telles and Ortiz 2008). In a study of Latino social values, majority of respondents believed that: (1) working hard is the path toward getting ahead in life, (2) one has to be very careful in dealings with others and can't be too trustful, and (3) religion is an important aspect of life (Taylor et al. 2012).

While there are strong similarities, Hispanic and Latino cultures can somewhat differ depending on their country of origin. As an example, while Hispanics share a cultural background, the extent of their identification with the Hispanic culture differs across ethnic groups (Villareal and Peterson 2008). With regard to personal perspectives on their culture, majority of Latino respondents indicated that (1) they believe they are of diverse cultures rather than a common culture, (2) they speak Spanish and view that it is important to continue the language into future generations to be continued into future generations, and (3) they identify themselves most with their country of origin rather than a pan-ethnic label (Taylor et al. 2012).

Hispanics and Latinos share a common perspective on the value America has provided to their lives and endeavors. A Pew Research Hispanic–Latino study indicated that (1) 87 percent of Latino adults believed that they had a better opportunity to get ahead in the United States than in their country of origin; (2) 72 percent of Latino indicated that the United States is a better environment for raising children than their home country; (3) 55 percent claimed they were as successful as other ethnic minority groups, 22 percent said they were less successful, and 17 percent believed they were more successful; and (4) 79 percent of Hispanic immigrants claimed that they would immigrate to the United States, if they had to do it over again (Taylor et al. 2012).

The Hispanic business community is large and growing. As of 2007, the number of Hispanic-owned businesses in the United States reached 2.3 million and posted a 43.7 percent increase in the period 2002 through 2007 (U.S. Census Bureau 2010).

Data supports the fact that the Hispanic community is a significant contributor to the U.S. economy. Hispanic-owned businesses generated $345.2 billion in sales in 2007, with a 55.5 percent increase from 2002. Approximately 44,206 Hispanic-owned businesses had receipts of $1 million or more. About 249,168 Hispanic-owned businesses have paid employees and employed 1.9 million people (U.S. Census Bureau 2010). Hispanics have a buying power of approximately $1.2 trillion (A.C. Nielsen 2013).

Some states in the United States have higher concentration of Hispanic entrepreneurs than others. States with the highest concentration of Hispanic business owners are: New Mexico (23.6 percent), Florida (22.4 percent), Texas (20.7 percent), California (16.5 percent), and Arizona (10.7 percent) (U.S. Census Bureau 2010).

Hispanic entrepreneurs have a diverse origin. Among Hispanic business owners, country or location of origin was as follows: Mexico (45.8 percent), Cuba (11.1 percent), Puerto Rico (6.9 percent), and people of other Hispanic origin (34.5 percent) (U.S. Census Bureau 2010).

There is, however, a lack of diversity in the types of business engaged by Hispanics. About one-third of Hispanic owned businesses were in construction repair and maintenance, personal services, and laundry industry. Personal services normally include skills that they leverage to earn some income such as haircutting, nail grooming, and the like. Industries such as wholesale, construction, and retail accounted for about 50 percent of Hispanic-owned business revenue (U.S. Census Bureau 2010).

While there has been a significant growth in the number of Hispanic businesses, there is much room for improvement. Hispanic businesses represent only about 7 percent of businesses in the United States (Barth, Yago, and Zeidman 2006).

The importance of the overall minority business in America is growing. A study by Lowrey (2004) showed that the share of minority owned businesses increased from 21 percent in 1982 to 32 percent in 2002. Minority firms generate over $920 billion in revenue and create jobs for over five million people (U.S. Census Bureau 2012).

As America is a melting pot of cultures, diverse businesses are started in the country. The outcome of these businesses can be shaped by their race (Fairlie and Robb 2007). Enz, Dollinger, and Daily (1990) found that organizational values of minority groups differed from those of non-minority groups.

It has been observed that in the context of business formation, minority groups are behind the majority groups (Kirchhoff, Stevens, and Hurwitz 1982). Business participation and income differ across ethnic groups (Fratoe 1986). Furthermore, business participation between native-born and immigrant populations also differ (Borjas 1986).

It is important to note that while minority firms constitute about 12 percent of U.S. businesses, their characteristics cannot be classified into one homogeneous sector (SBA 2005; Cardon et al. 2008). For instance, Scott (1983) observed that minority firms performed similarly to nonminority firms with regard to profitability, indebtedness, and liquidity.

Tienda and Raijman (2004) identified several reasons why native-born Hispanic entrepreneurs start their business. The reasons include: opportunity presented itself (34.2 percent), always wanted a business (34.2 percent), make more money (18.4 percent), desire for independence (18.4 percent), previous business experience (15.8 percent), had relevant skills (13.2 percent), difficulties in previous job (10.5 percent), and disadvantaged in U.S. market (5.3 percent).

Economic disadvantages stemming from unemployment, low wages, and discrimination lead to the pursuit of self-employment among minority entrepreneurs (Light 1979).

Motivation factors behind Hispanic entrepreneurship include financial gains, economic independence, adventure, power, prestige, and achievement (Raijman and Tienda 2000; Webber 1969).

Feldman, Koberg, and Dean (1991) observed that minority entrepreneurs (1) had higher education than the general minority population, (2) were confident and had a strong personality, and (3) they wanted to control their own destiny and sought achievement, power, and business success.

Characteristics

There are commonalities among minority enterprises. For instance, due to a variety of factors, many minority entrepreneurs are disadvantaged

(De Freitas 1991). Rogers et al. (2001) observed that firms owned by minority entrepreneurs were younger and smaller compared to those of nonminorities. Minority-owned firms tend to close shop and have lower survival rates as compared to nonminority enterprises (Boden and Headd 2002; Robb 2002). Munnell et al. (1996) observed that minority credit applicants were more likely to be rejected for mortgage loans than white applicants. Many minority entrepreneurs are driven to start their businesses because of need (Bates 1997). Minority owned businesses tend to be anchored on labor and positioned in low-growth sectors (Robb 2002). Minority firms tend to have lower probability of growth as compared to nonminority firms (Rogers et al. 2001).

Fairlie (2008) noted that immigrant entrepreneurship tend to be prevalent in areas with high volume of immigrants such as California, New York, New Jersey, and Florida. Many ethnic minority ventures are in retail and personal services (Rogers et al. 2001).

Minority entrepreneurs can experience tensions in finding work and family balance. In this group, the family unit is valued and is of primary importance in life (Lynch and Hanson 2004). In fact, many minority groups tend to have multigenerational and extended family households (Kamo 2000).

Minority entrepreneurs may experience high stress in their business endeavors. They tend to spend significant time in their business and have higher workload compared to traditional entrepreneurs (Harris, Saltstone, and Fraboni 1999).

There are difficulties faced with regard to finding the right kind of help. Minorities tend to have limited access to mentors (Ragins and Kram 2007).

Despite having commonalities in background, minority entrepreneurs are different from each other. Minority entrepreneurs have diverse views on motivations, satisfaction, and challenges experienced (Cardon et al. 2008).

Due to their background, experiences, and environment, Hispanic–Latino entrepreneurs have a distinct identity when conducting business.

Geographic location can have an impact on entrepreneurial disposition. Mexican immigrants situated in U.S. border cities tend to have higher incidences of self-employment potentially due to trade opportunities and competition in the labor market (Mora and Dávila 2006).

Relationships are often emphasized. Jones (1995) noted that there is propensity to prefer good working relationships and a professional work setting among Hispanic entrepreneurs.

Gender differences are evident. Shim and Eastlick (1998) noted differences among female and male Hispanic business owners in that females were (1) younger, (2) had less business experience, and (3) were likely not married. They also revealed that female owned Hispanic businesses were newer, had lesser people, and had lower annual sales than those of their male counterparts.

There is a preference to start rather than purchase a business. Tienda and Raijman (2004) noted that among native born Hispanic entrepreneurs a majority or 60.5 percent started a business, as compared to 26.3 percent who bought, and 13.2 percent who inherited. In an earlier study, Raijman and Tienda (2000) also observed that Hispanic entrepreneurs who had work experiences in a coethnic firm were more likely to start a business informally than those who did not work for a coethnic firm.

Hispanic entrepreneurs tend to draw upon their past work experiences when starting a business. Tienda and Raijman (2004) found that prior experience is key. In their study on native born Hispanic entrepreneurs, 81.3 percent claimed they had a salaried job prior to starting their current business. An even larger number or 92 percent claimed they acquired relevant business skills prior to starting their current business.

Feldman, Koberg, and Dean (1991) noted that minority entrepreneurs tend to be (1) young, (2) self-financed and collaborated with one or two financial partners, (3) engaged in a business where they had some experience, (4) left previous employment to start a business, and (5) aimed for stable growth.

Challenges

A myriad of factors lead to business challenges for Hispanic–Latino entrepreneurs. Hispanics were deeply impacted by the subprime crisis (Rivera et al. 2008). The economic recession had adverse impact on Latino men (Kochhar, Espinoza, and Hinze-Pifer 2010).

The environment and business factors can be deterrent. Fairlie and Woodruff (2006) noted lower business formation rates among Mexican entrepreneurs and non-Latino whites. A study by Lofstrom and Wang (2006) also noted that Mexican Hispanics were less likely to start a business than whites and were twice as likely to exit ownership in a business. Self-employment among male Mexican entrepreneurs is about 6 percent and is significantly lower than the 11 percent self-employment rate for the U.S. male population (Fairlie and Woodruff 2006).

Resource, education, and experiential inadequacies can dampen entrepreneurial drive. Hispanic households tend to be discouraged from applying for a loan (Crook 1996). Tienda and Raijman (2004) noted that among Hispanic entrepreneurs, lack of capital and knowledge on business formation can be deterrents to starting a business enterprise. Lofstrom and Wang (2006) attributed differences in tendency for business ownership among Hispanics and whites to education and wealth. Hispanics tend to have limited preownership experience (Shim and Eastlick 1998). Few Hispanics have parents who were engaged in business (Smith-Hunter 2006). Hispanic business owners may lack the human capital and business expertise such as marketing and finance to succeed in business (Dadzie and Cho 1989). Fairlie and Woodruff (2006) attributed lower Hispanic business formation to low education levels and limited financial resources among Mexican immigrants. Studies had shown that in the course of study, the dropout rates were higher for Latinos than for other racial groups (Snyder and Dillow 2011). Latino men tend to drop out when studying high school to join the workforce (Clark et al. 2008). Hispanic entrepreneurs tend to shy away from participating in training seminars and workshops (Gavino and Ortiz-Walters 2011).

Culture and circumstances can be business deterrents. For instance, Hispanic female entrepreneurs were more likely to turn to spouse or family for business advice rather than speaking with accountants or lawyers (Shim and Eastlick 1998). Minority entrepreneurs may have larger households than white counterparts and would likely have a higher incidence of single parenthood (U.S. Census Bureau 2007).

The type of industry a business is in can impact growth and work demand. Minority businesses tend to be labor heavy and positioned in industries with limited growth such as retail and personal services

(Robb 2002). Many minority businesses tend to have long hours and are driven by customer demands (Jennings and McDougald 2007).

Skillset limitations contribute to operational problems. Hispanic female entrepreneurs tend to face several business challenges such as forecasting sales, procuring lines of credit, financial management, and developing pricing strategies (Shim and Eastlick 1998). With identical attributes, Hispanic firms tend to have lower sales than non-Hispanic firms (Carvajal 2004)

There are several motivating factors. Mexican–American entrepreneurs may not necessarily have financial gains as their primary motivation. They tend to be motivated by prestige, power, and achievement, and not necessarily financial returns (Webber 1969). Vincent (1996) noted that Mexican–American entrepreneurs were less inclined to develop plans to assess business success or failure compared to their Anglo counterparts.

Opportunities

An entrepreneurial attitude and drive is present in the Hispanic–Latino community. This frame of mind combined with the right set of factors can lead to business success.

Tienda and Raijman (2004) observed that Hispanics tend to exhibit unique self-employment tendencies and entrepreneurial drive compared to other ethnic minorities. In a study exploring the motivation for immigration into the United States, 55 percent of Hispanics claimed it was for economic reasons, while 24 percent claimed it was for family reasons (Taylor et al. 2012). Patriarchal beliefs and cultural norms lead to unique demands on Latino men, especially with the need to be strong and provide for the needs of the family (Saenz and Ponjuan 2009).

The culture is one that has a strong work ethic. Mexican immigrants tend to work hard to gain some livelihood including informal forms of self-employment (Raijman 2001). Immigrants tend to be more mobile in their occupation than native workers as they pursue opportunities in diverse geographic locations, industries, and jobs (Orrenius and Zavodny 2009).

Entrepreneurial risk taking attitude is prevalent. Tienda and Raijman (2004) observed that native born Hispanic entrepreneurs may be willing to take risks for business gain. In their study, 44.7 percent were willing to risk their house to start a new business.

Propensity toward innovation and change is evident. Tienda and Raijman (2004) observed that native born Hispanic entrepreneurs seek ways to improve their business. In their study, when the entrepreneurs were asked to indicate their intent to change or innovate their business using a scale (1—keep business in place, 5—always think of ways to make business better), 86.9 percent rated themselves at 4 or 5.

Business cultivated through friendships and networks can further the agenda of the Hispanic–Latino entrepreneur. Entrepreneurial activities among immigrants often lead to job creation for new migrants (De Freitas 1991).

Cultivating a sense of community strengthens business foundations. Employment in coethnic firms encourages self-employment since it provides a venue for training and business preparation (Light et al. 1994). The accessibility of social resources such as credit, market access, and labor contributes to the success of ethnic enterprises (Lee et al. 1997).

While business challenges exist among Hispanic–Latino entrepreneurs, so do opportunities. Racial enclaves provide solidarity and enhance business development (Cummings 1980). With enhanced social networking and solidarity, ethnic groups gain abilities to better process information, expand financial capacity, strengthen market power, built trust, and build customer relationships (Light and Rosenstein 1995).

When resource obstacles are corrected, significant breakthroughs can take place. Immigrant entrepreneurs need to avoid "blocked opportunities" (Barrett, Jones, and McEvoy 1996).

Creative forms of social networking can help expand business operations. Minority and majority firm collaborations can be enhanced by initiatives such as joint ventures and alliances, creation of joint purchasing councils, establishment of information and clearing houses, roundtables, and directories (Lichtenstein and Lyons 1996).

While there have been numerous business successes among Hispanic–Latino entrepreneurs, there is still room for improvement. There are also opportunities to learn from the success of others and to find role models for current and future business.

Book Project Overview

While many of the current body of research on Hispanic–Latino entrepreneurship sheds light on the modalities, structure, and platform in which they operate, many of the studies tend to delve on the academic and quantitative aspects of research.

The authors noted the inadequacy of literature on qualitative studies on Hispanic–Latino entrepreneurship. Specifically, the authors found the need to dig deeper into how Hispanic–Latino entrepreneurs think and what led to their business success.

In this book, the authors spent two years gathering profiles and viewpoints of the leading Hispanic–Latino entrepreneurs in America. A questionnaire was developed and interviews conducted via e-mail, mail, telephone, and face-to-face.

For the purpose of this research endeavor and book project, Hispanic–Latino refer to men and women who are of Hispanic or Latino origin and are currently engaged in business in America and are American citizens. There were no further qualifications.

The entrepreneurs interviewed were selected based on success in their field and industry. While a question on their financial standing was not asked, it is easy to establish from their profile and accomplishments that these individuals are active and practicing entrepreneurs in their own right. They have not only survived but succeeded in America's tough and challenging business environment.

The intent of the authors was to get to know the Hispanic–Latino entrepreneur better and let them tell their story. The authors made an effort to uncover aspects such as (1) how they started their business, (2) how they overcame business challenges, and (3) what strategies they employed to succeed in America.

The authors developed a 15-item questionnaire specially designed to extract the information they needed and encourage the entrepreneurs to openly discuss what they think on the subject.

The number of questions was limited due to sensitivity to the time availability and schedule of these busy entrepreneurs.

The end product of this research effort is a limited but profound compilation of the profiles and viewpoints of typical Hispanic–Latino entrepreneurs across different locations in America. These are regular business people who get up to work every day and contribute to the economic engine of the country.

It is the hope of the authors that this body of work will serve as an inspiration to young entrepreneurs and the Hispanic–Latino community.

In the concluding chapter, the authors discuss the common threads in the interview responses and what this means to the understanding and appreciation of Hispanic–Latino entrepreneurship.

This research project is valuable to the academic community, the business sector, and the government and policy makers. The academic community would find the profiles and interviews useful in case studies on entrepreneurship and other business discussions. The business sector would find value in the biographical information provided on typical Hispanic–Latino entrepreneurs. The lessons and advice the entrepreneurs generously offer can serve as a roadmap for business success in America. These lessons are valuable to would-be entrepreneurs, struggling entrepreneurs, minority entrepreneurs, and the broader business community. Government organizations and policy makers would find value in the candid commentaries of the entrepreneurs on topics such as education, training, and networking.

Project Support and Impact

The authors wish to point out that the profiles were provided by the interviewed entrepreneurs. The demographic information provided was gathered based on trust and was not validated. The authors are confident that the interviewees were sincere in providing all information. The interview feedback and commentaries offered by the entrepreneurs were from their own words and writing or were confirmed accurate by them. In a few instances, the text was rephrased or slightly edited to enhance the clarity of message. While all participating entrepreneurs are duly acknowledged, their specific responses to the questions are concealed as a respect for privacy. The authors specifically mention the industry they are associated with to provide context to the readers.

This book project would not be possible without the help and support of countless individuals. The authors wish to thank several students at the

Tabor School of Business at Millikin University especially Ryan Abernathy, Frank Byers, Caleb Buscher, Natalie Canham, Manny Chacon, Heather Gilmore, Ruth Goddard, Kevin Gottlieb, Andrew Hendrian, Katie Mulderink, Eric Tobey, and Stephawn Woodley. Exceptionally helpful to this research project was Jamie Rockhold who diligently assisted in several interviews, assembled numerous research data, and contributed to the writing of the manuscript and analysis. This project would not have been possible without Jamie's hardwork and support.

With regard to the book structure, the authors feature the interviews at random. Overview and discussion of the findings are offered in the first and last chapters.

On a personal note, the authors found this research journey to be heartwarming and inspirational. In the course of three years, the authors have found not just highly cooperative interviewees but lifelong friends. Despite their impressive accomplishments and success, the interviewees remained humble and well-grounded. There is much to be admired about Hispanic–Latino entrepreneurship.

Finally, the authors wish that this book will be a source of inspiration to the reader and will serve as a key to unlock the doors to entrepreneurial success in America.

CHAPTER 2

Nature of the Study

There are several reasons why the authors conducted this research study. Topping the list is the desire to understand the psyche of the Hispanic–Latino entrepreneur.

Specifically, the authors wanted to know: What makes the Hispanic–Latino entrepreneur tick? What were the motivations for success? What challenges were faced? How did they overcome the challenges? What is their story?

Since literature on the subject was scarce, the authors had to conduct personal interviews. It would not be possible to interview all successful Hispanic–Latino entrepreneurs in America, so the authors reached out to who they could.

The interviewees came from all walks of life. Some ran established businesses, others were just starting out. Some were seasoned businessmen, others were young entrepreneurs. Some were highly educated, others were not. Essentially, the interviewees comprised of the typical real-life Hispanic–Latino entrepreneurs in the United States.

An effort was placed to gather viewpoints from diverse industries and geographical locations across the United States.

The authors aimed to gather at least 20 fully completed interviews. In the end, 25 questionnaires were collected, and 20 were deemed complete and are featured in this book.

The authors conducted the interviews in order to examine commonalities in thinking and approaches. The idea is not to bundle together or generalize Hispanic–Latino attitudes, but to examine if the success strategies could also work for other would-be entrepreneurs.

During the course of the interviews, it soon became evident that responses to each question tended to be different. Each entrepreneur processed the questions and articulated their thoughts in a different and distinct manner. Answers came from different directions and emerged from diverse paths. In essence, each interview was unique.

While this development made the uncovering of commonalities challenging, it spoke volumes of the high level of individuality of the Hispanic–Latino entrepreneur. They were their own story.

While the answers were not always similar, the questions were standardized. The authors refrained from deviating from the original set of questions except in cases where clarity was essential. The authors also refrained from extracting personal information as a respect to privacy.

In the table, the authors list the 15 questions asked and highlight the rationale for each question.

Questions	Rationale
Kindly provide an overview of your family history. For example, was there an entrepreneur in your family? Did your family history influence your decision to start a business?	To uncover if the family influenced the entrepreneurial decision. Some studies seem to suggest this fact, the authors wanted to validate if this is the case with Hispanic–Latino entrepreneurs.
What was your educational background? Do you have specific views on formal versus informal education? What are your views on Hispanic–Latino entrepreneurial training programs? Has education contributed to your business success?	To understand the role education played in the entrepreneurial decision and success. The authors also wanted to gain insights whether formal or informal education is preferable.
Everyone has at least one role model, someone they aspire to be like. Do you have one who is an entrepreneur? How did the role model(s) influence your decision to start a business?	To understand who the entrepreneurial role models are and the role they played in stimulating business interest.
Starting a new business is not an easy process. What motivated you to start one? What steps did you take to start the business?	To uncover motivations behind the entrepreneurial start-up.
What challenges did you face when building your business, and how did you overcome them? Did you come across any unique circumstances as a result of your race?	To explore challenges faced when starting a business enterprise and approaches taken to deal with the challenges. The authors wanted to know whether there were racial barriers that the Hispanic–Latino entrepreneurs needed to overcome.

Questions	Rationale
What types of support were most helpful to you when you were building your business? For example, did your local community play a role in shaping your business interests and development, or maybe it was a mentor? What or who was the one thing that made you believe, "Yes, I can do this!"	To learn about the types of business support most beneficial to Hispanic–Latinos when they build their business. The authors wanted to know whether mentors, organizations, or the local community contributed to business growth.
What do you think are the essential skills needed for Hispanic–Latino entrepreneurs to succeed in America? Also, what personal attitudes do you think are essential?	To determine what skills and attributes are essential for Hispanic–Latino business success in America. The authors were hoping to identify attitudes and values that could be cultivated among the youth and future entrepreneurs.
If you had the chance to start over again, would you do anything differently? If so, what's the reason?	To gain an understanding on entrepreneurial challenges and mistakes and what can be improved.
How would you characterize the state of Hispanic–Latino entrepreneurship in the United States? For instance, is it in the early stages, is it growing, or is it mature? Do you think it is open to all, or limited to certain individuals? Is it viable from anywhere in the country, or more favorable in certain states?	To gain an understanding of the overall status of Hispanic–Latino entrepreneurship in the United States. The authors wanted to know whether entrepreneurship is for a privileged few or open to everybody. The authors also wanted to gain insights whether certain states present entrepreneurial advantages.
Are you a member of business organizations? Are these organizations unique to Hispanic–Latinos or open to all races? Did they contribute to your business success?	To uncover the role business organizations play in the success of Hispanic–Latino entrepreneurs.
Do you think social networks and personal connections are important to business? Did you use networking when building your business, and are your social networks race based?	To uncover the role social networks and connections play in the success of Hispanic–Latino entrepreneurs. The authors also wanted to understand if race played a role in their networking activities.
If you could give advice to young Hispanic–Latino entrepreneurs or other young people thinking about starting a business, what would be the most important consideration and why?	To gain additional insights that may be helpful to the Hispanic–Latino youth and future entrepreneurs.
Have you been involved in sociocivic organizations or philanthropic work? If so, in which organizations, and what role did you play?	To understand the extent of sociocivic involvement and community outreach among Hispanic–Latino entrepreneurs.

(Continued)

(*Continued*)

Questions	Rationale
What do you see happening to your business in the future? Do you have succession plans in place? Do you see your business being run by family members or professional managers, and why?	To examine the extent of forward thinking and succession planning among Hispanic–Latino entrepreneurs. The authors also wanted to determine whether the entrepreneurs tend to involve family members in their business and reasons behind their decisions.
Where do you see yourself 10 years from now? What do you think is your legacy to the business community?	To understand the dreams and aspirations of Hispanic–Latino entrepreneurs. The authors also wanted to see the kind of legacy the entrepreneurs wish to leave behind and how they want to be remembered.

The interviews conducted were both complete and inadequate. They were complete in a sense that all the 15 questions were asked and answered. They were inadequate because there are more questions to be asked. It seemed like there is much more to be learned about Hispanic–Latino entrepreneurship. Regretfully, there were project timelines and resource limitations to live with.

Nevertheless, the authors believe that the compiled interviews present an exciting business perspective of Hispanic–Latino entrepreneurs in the New Millennium. These interviews are the first of its kind and will hopefully open the doors to similar studies in the future. The answers to the questions present insights that are valuable to students and researchers, as well as entrepreneurs. Countless lessons are offered in each entrepreneurial story.

In the next chapter, the entrepreneurial stories are introduced, and the mystery behind Hispanic–Latino entrepreneurship is unraveled.

CHAPTER 3

The Hispanic–Latino Entrepreneurs

In this section, the viewpoints of Hispanic–Latino entrepreneurs are offered. Specific names accompanying the interviews were omitted as a way of respecting personal privacy.

The authors wish to thank the following contributors for generously sharing their time and their views: (alphabetically) Geromino Chacon, Leslie Class, Tony Calderon, Michael Fernandez, David Fuentes, Sammy Garduno, Sylvia Klinger, Manuel Leon, Lu Camarena Meshulam, Francisco Negrete, Ruben Orozco, Ray Padron, Valeria Pasmanter, Valentin Rios, Jacqueline Rivera, Michelle Sanchez, Raul Soto, Miguel Tapia, Alex Torrenegra, and Eduardo Torres.

The insights provided constitute the views of the respondents and do not necessarily imply a shared view of the authors. The respondents were invited to share their honest and candid perceptions on the subject.

The featured interviews are current and real-life. These are not the views of researchers but actual practitioners of Hispanic–Latino entrepreneurship.

The authors hope that our significant investment of time, energy, and resources to enhance the understanding of Hispanic–Latino entrepreneurship will lead to a deeper knowledge of the subject. Moreover, we hope that these interviews will inspire others to follow the path of these successful role models.

Project Contractor

Interview

1. Here we ask you to provide us an overview of your family history. For example, was there an entrepreneur in your family? Did your family history influence your decision to start a business?

   I am originally from Mexico. My family was poor. My father was skilled in carpentry so he taught us how to make things. We made cabinets, beds, windows, furniture, and many other things. We began a family business in Mexico making furniture. My dad also taught me mechanical work, electric, plumbing, and construction. My mother soon opened a store where she sold everyday necessities. I came to the United States to help my family financially because with 10 kids and my parents, we did not make enough. I began working construction in the United States, mainly drywall. I became skilled enough that I decided to go into business on my own. I started my company and invested in everything I needed and started looking for contractors. Now, my company is successful and work is stable.

2. What was your educational background? Do you have specific views on formal versus informal education? What are your views on Hispanic–Latino entrepreneurial training programs? Has education contributed to your business success?

   I went to school. I made it through middle school but I did not continue on to high school or college. The best education I received was hands on with my father. I learned so many things that I use today. I do not have specific views on formal and informal education. I am proof that whether or not you have an education, you can still make something of yourself. I think that Hispanic–Latino entrepreneurial training programs are great. A lot of Hispanics come from countries where education is not the best and due to poverty it is really hard to continue education because the children need to work to help bring income for necessities. These training programs allow Hispanics to learn and make a better life for themselves. I would say education has contributed to my business success. A hand on experience has allowed me to learn and get better at what I do. I also continued to study things here in the United States on my own, and I have learned a lot of things that will make me successful. I am going to continue to certifications and licenses.

3. Everyone has at least one role model, someone they aspire to be like. Do you have one who is an entrepreneur? How did they influence your decision to start a business?

My role model by far was my father. He worked his entire life to provide for me, my mother, and my siblings. My father was an entrepreneur. He created furniture and hoped that he would sell it. He took a risk, invested, and succeeded. I saw what my dad did and it made me want to be as hard working. I saw that a person could do a lot more by owning their own business despite the risk or investment it took. That is why I started my business.

4. Starting a new business isn't something people take lightly. Why did you start yours? What steps did you take to start the business?

I started my own business to help my family. I gave my brothers work and was able to create an extra income. I had to get the business license, FIN, insurance, and publicize the name before I could begin. I also had to invest in tools, material, and workers.

5. What challenges did you face when building your business, and how did you overcome them? Did you come across any unique circumstances as a result of your race?

The challenges I faced were many. I was faced with competition, environmental issues, lack of laborers, mistakes, etc. I overcame these by finding a solution, one by one. I looked in other areas for work. I found a way to overcome weather issue. I hired my brothers, and I learned from my mistakes.

There were no unique circumstances because of this. Just like any other entrepreneur, I was challenged and I succeeded.

6. What types of support were most helpful to you when you were building your business? For example, did your local community play a role in shaping your business interests and development, or maybe

it was a mentor? What or who was the one thing that made you believe, "Yes, I can do this!"

I had a lot of help from my family. My brothers helped me work, my parents supported me and gave me a reason to push forward, and help from friends who already had experience. My family was my number one mentor.

7. What do you think are the essential skills needed for Hispanic–Latino entrepreneurs to succeed in America? Also, what personal attitudes do you think are essential?

I think what is essential is an education. Knowing how to read, write, and speak the English language is the only thing that will make you successful as a Latino in America. A positive, optimistic attitude is important. If you keep telling yourself you will succeed, you will. A negative attitude will hold you back. You also need to be friendly natured and have great communication skills.

8. If you had the chance to start over again, would you do anything differently? More to the point, if you would, what's the reason?

I think my only mistake is not having enough workers. I would not go back and change anything though. My business is a success because regardless of what obstacle I faced, I accomplished it.

9. How would you characterize the state of Hispanic–Latino entrepreneurship in the United States? For instance, is it in the early stages, is it growing, or is it mature? Do you think it is open to all, or limited to certain individuals? Is it viable from anywhere in the country, or more favorable in certain states?

A lot of Hispanics and Latinos are starting businesses in the United States and are bettering themselves and our economy. Quite a few started early with the essentials they needed, so their business is growing rapidly. There are still many that are just starting out in the early stages to see if it is going to work. I don't know of any businesses that are in the mature stage and will not continue to grow. It is definitely open to all individuals. No matter who you are, you can do something if you put the time and effort in. The entire country is booming with Hispanic–Latino entrepreneurs. There are states where more Hispanic businesses are located, but it also has to do with State laws.

10. Are you a member of business organizations? Are these organizations unique to Hispanic–Latinos or open to all races? Did they contribute to your business success?

    I am not a member of any business organization. There are organizations out there, but they are directed at all races.

11. Do you think social networks and personal connections are important to business? Did you use networking when building your business, and are your social networks race based?

    Absolutely. Word of mouth is the best advertising there is. It is what has made me a success. Social networks reach millions of people near and far and create opportunities everywhere. I did use networking to build my business. My social networks were not race based. I did have mostly Spanish speaking friends because of the language barrier, but it was never race based.

12. If you could give advice to young Hispanic–Latino entrepreneurs or other young people thinking about starting a business, what would be the most important thing, and why?

    The most important thing is to take the risk. You never know if you can succeed if you do not try. There is risk and investment in every success. A lot of people are held back because they don't want to risk failure, but it is what makes you stronger and persevere in the end.

13. Have you been involved in sociocivic organizations or philanthropic work? If so, in which organizations, and what role did you play?

    No.

14. What do you see happening to your business in the future? Do you have succession plans in place? Do you see your business being run by family members or professional managers, and why?

I see my business expanding and growing in size. My succession plan is already in place. My business is run by family members. They will always be my administration. They know about the business and have worked in it from the start. They are people I trust and I cannot go wrong with family.

15. Where do you see yourself 10 years from now?

Ten years from now I see myself heading the company with at least a dozen workers. I would like to create employment for others. I see my company being big with work all over Illinois and surrounding states.

16. What do you think is your legacy to the business community?

My legacy is all of the buildings I have helped build; the lives I have changed; the jobs I have created; and the name that will last forever because of hard work and dedication.

Healthcare Entrepreneur

Interview

1. Here we ask you to provide us an overview of your family history. For example, was there an entrepreneur in your family? Did your family history influence your decision to start a business?

My father arrived here from Puerto Rico. He had a poor upbringing and subsequently joined the U.S. Army. When he left the Army, he partnered up with a Jewish fellow and started an electrical company. The company became very successful and made millions. When I was young, I used to go around with him when he was working, and he always introduced me as his "little assistant." This entrepreneurial exposure early shaped my interest. My father did what he wanted to do, and did not want to work for anyone. I am that way too.

2. What was your educational background? Do you have specific views on formal versus informal education? What are your views on Hispanic–Latino entrepreneurial training programs? Has education contributed to your business success?

While I have been known to be a bright person at school, I have had educational challenges. I dropped out of school at about 16. Family circumstances and a feeling that it wasn't challenging enough led to the dropping out. At one point, I took the General Education Development (GED) test and got a high score. Subsequently, I finished two years of high school at a residential facility. I do think schooling is very important. I am a rare case. I don't recommend dropping out of school. It's a very competitive environment out there. It's going to be even harder to succeed without good education. In my case, I was not aware nor was I able to take advantage of entrepreneurial training programs that helped me.

3. Everyone has at least one role model, someone they aspire to be like. Do you have one who is an entrepreneur? How did they influence your decision to start a business?

My father was my primary role model in life. He helped a lot of people and changed their lives for the better. In many ways, his attitude has shaped my business mindset and the way I do business. My business allows me to teach others and I enjoy doing it and watch lives get transformed.

4. Starting a new business isn't something people take lightly. Why did you start yours? What steps did you take to start the business?

I started my paramedical business while working full time. I've always multi-tasked throughout my life—working two or three jobs at a time. While working on a job, I did business on the side to see if the model works. Later on, I had the idea to start a school and went for it. I gave myself six months to make it work. Fortunately, I was able to successfully grow my client base and was able to work full time in my school.

5. What challenges did you face when building your business, and how did you overcome them? Did you come across any unique circumstances as a result of your race?

The primary challenge I faced was financial. I needed money to buy supplies and equipment. I overcame this challenge by working 14 hour days. In my other job, I worked as independent contractor. The more hours I worked, the more I earned. So, I simply worked harder and longer to have money for the school. It's tough—at times I feel burned out, but I am motivated by the thought that many people depend on me and I am recognized for my efforts. Thus far, race has never been an issue for me or my business. I simply don't allow it.

6. What types of support were most helpful to you when you were building your business? For example, did your local community play a role in shaping your business interests and development, or maybe it was a mentor? What or who was the one thing that made you believe, "Yes, I can do this!"

A number of business organizations helped me. In my business, I approached several nonprofit organizations and several of them supported me. A community center offered to host the school as an operating venue and helped in advertising. This support helped me keep my expenses in check. It allows me to offer my courses cheap and accessible to my low-income customers. Support from my family played an important role as well. They believed in me and encouraged me not to quit. Through their support, I was able to keep my business growing for the past six years. I was able to do research, develop the curriculum, and expand my customer base.

7. What do you think are the essential skills needed for Hispanic–Latino entrepreneurs to succeed in America? Also, what personal attitudes do you think are essential?

A very strong desire to see their work through to the end is essential. They need to be able to overcome all challenges. Never quit. Go all the way. Believe in yourself. All these will pave the way for success.

8. If you had the chance to start over again, would you do anything differently? More to the point, if you would, what's the reason?

I'm a big believer that everything happens for a reason. In my case, if things were easier, I would not be as passionate in my work. Challenges make you stronger. They push you to improve what you do. I enjoy challenges. I believe without struggles, I couldn't figure out my way.

9. How would you characterize the state of Hispanic–Latino entrepreneurship in the United States? For instance, is it in the early stages, is it growing, or is it mature? Do you think it is open to all, or limited

to certain individuals? Is it viable from anywhere in the country, or more favorable in certain states?

The state of Hispanic–Latino entrepreneurship in the States is still in the early stages. The younger generation holds a lot of promise. They are highly Americanized and don't consider race to be an issue. They view themselves as equal to all other races. This is the new way of the world. There is less and less segregation. There is more equality. The younger generation tends to pursue their preferred career interest and start their own businesses. They figure out a way to make things work. They have a high potential to be successful. And this trend is just starting and will continue to grow.

The opportunities for entrepreneurship tend to be more abundant in more metropolitan areas. In these locations, more program assistance and other forms of support are available. In these locations, there are more program initiators and active leaders who make things happen.

10. Are you a member of business organizations? Are these organizations unique to Hispanic–Latinos or open to all races? Did they contribute to your business success?

I'm currently not a member of a business organization, but am currently looking to be more involved. I have spent the past few years just focused on the business and helping it grow. Some organizations charge steep fees and this has somewhat discouraged me from being involved.

11. Do you think social networks and personal connections are important to business? Did you use networking when building your business, and are your social networks race based?

Personal connections are extremely important, specially, when you are growing a business. In recent years, I have done more to optimize the use of social networking. It's an excellent tool, especially, if you have a limited budget.

12. If you could give advice to young Hispanic–Latino entrepreneurs or other young people thinking about starting a business, what would be the most important thing, and why?

It's not as easy as you think. You have to be innovative and continually think outside the box. There's a lot of competing small businesses out there. It is easy to start, it is highly replicable. Your business really has to be unique. While similar business models are out there, you have to find a way to make it your own.

13. Have you been involved in sociocivic organizations or philanthropic work? If so, in which organizations, and what role did you play?

   Not really, also the work I do is really socially focused. It's like I do philanthropy every day.

14. What do you see happening to your business in the future? Do you have succession plans in place? Do you see your business being run by family members or professional managers, and why?

   I hope to eventually evolve into a nonprofit organization so that I can qualify for funding for my programs. I currently rely on student tuition. Having access to other funding sources can help my business grow to the level I want. I'd like to expand the business to other locations, such as Florida. Eventually, I'd also like to expand my program offering and make a deeper impact on the lives of my customers.

15. Where do you see yourself 10 years from now?

   Hopefully, running a successful and sustainable business. I love what I do and enjoy working for myself. I'd like to just keep doing it.

16. What do you think is your legacy to the business community?

   I'd like to share the story of my life to others. Let them know that one should never give up on your dreams. Follow your desired path, and shape your destiny.

Model Agency Owner and Artist

Interview

1. Here we ask you to provide us an overview of your family history. For example, was there an entrepreneur in your family? Did your family history influence your decision to start a business?

   There have been no entrepreneurs in my family. My mother had entrepreneurial characteristics and I learned a lot from her. I almost pursued a career as a teacher. In fact, I received a lot of encouragement to pursue a career in teaching. But, decided to change paths. I certainly do not regret it. I did not get support from my family in the beginning. We were brought up to be employees. But I'm glad I did it. I ended up being the first entrepreneur in the family.

2. What was your educational background? Do you have specific views on formal versus informal education? What are your views on Hispanic–Latino entrepreneurial training programs? Has education contributed to your business success?

I graduated with a marketing degree at the University of Texas at El Paso. Prior to that, I had an Associate degree in Liberal Arts at El Paso Community College. In my view, business school education is valuable. Business classes tend to be more useful in business rather than Astronomy or Calculus. I was fortunate to receive an entrepreneurship scholarship from the Dallas Hispanic Chamber. I was able to enhance my business skills from the training I received.

3. Everyone has at least one role model, someone they aspire to be like. Do you have one who is an entrepreneur? How did they influence your decision to start a business?

I need to give this some more thought. I mostly relied on myself and not so much on role models to achieve the goals I aspired for.

4. Starting a new business isn't something people take lightly. Why did you start yours? What steps did you take to start the business?

I had no initial plan to start a business. It happened through a partnership after we spotted an opportunity. As the business grew, we eventually parted ways and I went on my own. I subsequently expanded my business as new opportunities emerged.

5. What challenges did you face when building your business, and how did you overcome them? Did you come across any unique circumstances as a result of your race?

The challenges I faced were mostly not attributable to race. It's more attributable to the fact that I was a woman. I was also quite young looking. And, business people tended not to take me seriously. Further-more, most of my clients were male. I had to make an effort to prove myself and really show them what I was capable of. In my business, you need to be tough and can't be too nice.

6. What types of support were most helpful to you when you were building your business? For example, did your local community play a role in shaping your business interests and development, or maybe it was a mentor? What or who was the one thing that made you believe, "Yes, I can do this!"

I really started my business from scratch. I kept my expenses low and even used credit cards to stay afloat. I took advantage of an incuba-tor program. I was able to use a proper business space at a low cost. I did most of my business from my website. I did a lot of networking. Also, I did a lot of trading—trading my services for other products and services. I still do this today—leverage what I have and swap with others to conserve cash flow. It works very well.

I received help from people, but mostly had to rely on myself. There are a handful of people at the Chamber that were helpful, including a coach and mentor. However, it was ultimately up to me to make things happen.

In my case, I was not quite exposed to the community to gain support. Incidentally, one amusing thing is that other ethnic communities tend to support my efforts. I get a lot of support from the Indian, Pakistani, and other ethnic groups. They tend to look at me as one of them. In some of these cultures, women are not too involved in entertainment and related kinds of businesses, and they have accepted me as one of their own. In my Facebook page for instance, I have followers now from many parts of the world.

7. What do you think are the essential skills needed for Hispanic–Latino entrepreneurs to succeed in America? Also, what personal attitudes do you think are essential?

The key skill sets are

> *Perseverance: Keep at it despite the obstacles;*
> *Personality: Have the right image and attitude;*

Independence: Rely on yourself, can't depend on anybody;

Networking ability: Build your contacts and develop relationships;

Adapt and reinvent: Be prepared to shift gears as new opportunities arise;

Leadership: Business people need to be able to lead, otherwise you are doomed to fail. You need to be able to motivate people to do things.

8. If you had the chance to start over again, would you do anything differently? More to the point, if you would, what's the reason?

I would likely go the same route. If there's anything I would change, it would be to get more people involved. When starting the business, I did everything myself. At some point, I got burned out working very hard to prove that my vision was right. Not many people believed in me. It was only on the fourth year when people wanted to be involved. It may have been better if I got more people involved early.

9. How would you characterize the state of Hispanic–Latino entrepreneurship in the United States? For instance, is it in the early stages, is it growing, or is it mature? Do you think it is open to all, or limited to certain individuals? Is it viable from anywhere in the country, or more favorable in certain states?

The state of Hispanic–Latino entrepreneurship in America still has a long way to go. There's still a lot of room for growth. The past generation has been prepared to be employees. This is now changing. The newer generation is better prepared and see exciting opportunities in top careers and business. For instance, emerging opportunities are opening up in the nonprofit space.

In Dallas, Hispanic–Latino entrepreneurship is expanding. It's at a stage that's not in the beginning stages, more like the middle stages, with lots of opportunities for the future.

The state of entrepreneurship is also changing. It has evolved due to new economic situations. People are having new mindsets. It's a great time to make a go for it. Whatever race you are, if you have the potential, start something. There are a lot of opportunities out there, specially, in the bigger cities. There are many programs that support entrepreneurship. Take advantage of these programs.

10. Are you a member of business organizations? Are these organizations unique to Hispanic–Latinos or open to all races? Did they contribute to your business success?

I belong to the Hispanic Chamber and soon will be Women Business Certified. The business organizations can help to some extent, but in my case I did most of the pushing and networking to get the business to grow.

11. Do you think social networks and personal connections are important to business? Did you use networking when building your business, and are your social networks race based?

As previously mentioned, social networks and personal connections are critical to business success—regardless of race.

It's never about the race. Networks reach out to everybody—pursue your dreams. In my case, social media has become a valuable tool. I spend several hours on Facebook each day. I now have a fan and contact base in excess of five thousand and growing. It's a great marketing tool to grow your business.

12. If you could give advice to young Hispanic–Latino entrepreneurs or other young people thinking about starting a business, what would be the most important thing, and why?

Believe in yourself. Even your family may not believe in you. Without personal faith and confidence, you would not survive.

13. Have you been involved in sociocivic organizations or philanthropic work? If so, in which organizations, and what role did you play?

I have been previously involved in a mentoring program. I found the program to be underdeveloped and had limitations on mentoring. It was also bent on money and donations. I have opted to create my own. I started a mentoring program as a way of mentoring others in a very meaningful manner.

14. What do you see happening to your business in the future? Do you have succession plans in place? Do you see your business being run by family members or professional managers, and why?

I'm expanding. I've launched a new line to include marketing, branding, social media, and management. I work with smaller client, and work with their budget.

In my business, I try to keep my family away. They also live far away from me. I wish I could get my mom involved though. I have learned a lot from her.

15. Where do you see yourself 10 years from now?

My goal is to eventually have an operating partner for my business. Someone who can help run the business. I plan to eventually settle down and have a family. The routine I had in the past years have been extremely hectic. I hardly have a personal life. It was difficult to develop and maintain a relationship. I have to make changes down the road.

16. What do you think is your legacy to the business community?

I hope to be remembered as a role model to the Hispanic–Latino community. Right now, I have a large, loyal audience through Facebook. Many have become friends and they value my correspondences and business. They even remember suggestions, and the advice I gave weeks or months ago. Many look up to me. I can't give up and let them down. I work hard to ensure my business succeeds for a long time.

Food Industry and Health Consultant

Interview

1. Here we ask you to provide us an overview of your family history. For example, was there an entrepreneur in your family? Did your family history influence your decision to start a business?

My parents were not entrepreneurs, they were missionaries. However, for some reason, my siblings and I ended up in entrepreneurial careers. I still maintain a missionary mindset in my business though. I devote about 60 percent of my time helping others.

One strong influence my parents had on me was to value education. My parents were both first in their family to go to college. They viewed education as a gift to me. I believe education is a framework for success. Through education one can earn a salary or start a business—and have a life that's different and better.

Another influence my parents had on me was drive—a passion to work hard, continue to grow, and manage changes.

A few mentors helped along the way. They helped build trust and developed my confidence to really do something.

2. What was your educational background? Do you have specific views on formal versus informal education? What are your views on Hispanic–Latino entrepreneurial training programs? Has education contributed to your business success?

I was born in Puerto Rico and grew up in Mexico. When I first arrived in America, I hardly spoke English. Yet, I made an effort to get a college degree. I managed to get a bachelor's degree in nutrition and dietetics at Loma Linda University in California. I worked for a few years and got a master's degree in public service administration at De Paul University in Chicago.

Years ago, there were not much formal and informal entrepreneurial training opportunities for the Latino community. I was not able to take advantage of such programs. I do see the benefits of such programs, however, it can really help individuals who want to do something with their lives.

There is a high demand and interest for entrepreneurial training in the Latino community. In fact, I know colleagues who take advantage of sales training provided by organizations such as Amway to learn basic selling and business skills.

3. Everyone has at least one role model, someone they aspire to be like. Do you have one who is an entrepreneur? How did they influence your decision to start a business?

I have several role models. One is Oprah Winfrey. I admire the way she does business. She treats people well and genuinely cares for them. She is always ready to offer a helping hand. She would say things like "Let's sit down and have coffee together. Talk to me. How can I help you? How can I make your life better?" I embrace this philosophy and apply in my business. It's also a typical outlook in the Latino community. It's hardly about the money—it's about how people are treated. People stay with you and work with you because you treat them well.

I also admire Mother Teresa. She gave love and kindness—unconditionally.

My parents have been my role models too. They sold their cars and homes to give me and my brother the education we needed. This sacrifices and unconditional love sticks with me. Every day, it drives me to be successful. I want to always give my best and go all out—to make their sacrifices worthwhile.

4. Starting a new business isn't something people take lightly. Why did you start yours? What steps did you take to start the business?

I started my business after I was laid off many years ago. I worked for a multinational corporation and was laid off after 10 years in the company. I was one of the later ones to be let go. I never thought I'd be one of them. I went home crying and crying. In the end, it was the best thing that ever happened to me. The day after I was laid off, a company executive called and asked whether I could finish some pending project in a consulting capacity. One consulting project led to others—mostly by word of mouth. Eventually my consulting practice grew. After a few years, several other large multinational companies started to give me projects as well.

I started with very little capital. I leveraged my skills and abilities. It didn't matter whether I was Latino or not. Many of my clients even love the accent!

When I was starting, everything was built by word of mouth. I didn't even have a cell phone until years later. I didn't have corporate brochures or any fancy marketing tool.

My consulting practice grew mostly as a result of my reputation. My ability to work hard and deliver value to my clients.

With little resources, I was able to develop a website and the business continued to grow. The website was even developed under a trade arrangement. I offered discounted service to a client in exchange for his helping me set up the site. I also had to balance my time managing the business and looking after the children. At times, I worked on the projects at midnight when the children were asleep. It was only in later years, when I could afford to hire people.

As my business grew, it gave me confidence. It built my self-esteem. I started to realize that I do have something to offer that was valuable to my clients.

5. What challenges did you face when building your business, and how did you overcome them? Did you come across any unique circumstances as a result of your race?

A significant challenge is that people took their time to pay me. I had traveling and other expenses and payment came months later. One really has to be savvy about financial matters. When you get a check, it doesn't automatically mean you can spend the money. There should always be some financial cushion—in the event that payments do come late. I don't like to call clients every week to collect a check. I'd prefer to have a financial cushion to be able to follow up after a few weeks. It is more professional.

In my consulting practice, I also have to be careful that I don't come across any conflict of interest. I make an effort to be honest and maintain a high level of integrity.
One challenge is how to balance work and family. I try not to spread myself thin in important aspects of my life.

6. What types of support were most helpful to you when you were building your business? For example, did your local community play a role in shaping your business interests and development, or maybe it was a mentor? What or who was the one thing that made you believe, "Yes, I can do this!"

My immediate friends helped me a lot. They cheered me on and boosted my confidence. They used to kid me by saying "you have the best job in the world! You do your business at the comfort of your home, at any time you want!"

My parents played a role. They continue to inspire me. During important meetings, my mom makes an effort to know the details of the meeting. She always tells me that she'll be praying for me.

Friendships on a professional level is important. The friendships you develop help out. Word gets around. People remember you and help out where they can. That's why it's important to build a good reputation. With regard to my projects, I make it a point to deliver on time and exceed client expectations. I keep a high standard. I always want to bring in some value added—to knock the ball out of the ballpark.

7. What do you think are the essential skills needed for Hispanic–Latino entrepreneurs to succeed in America? Also, what personal attitudes do you think are essential?

Honesty and values. Latinos bring a lot to business—we are bilingual, we show a lot of caring, and have strong and positive values. We need to cherish our heritage and continue to be helpful to others. Use these values to be productive.

We should continue building upon our integrity.

We need to be flexible, and always be ready to change and evolve. We need to be open-minded.

We need to be people-oriented and learn to be good team players. It's important to remember that you can never do business alone. You need people to help you. I am indebted to many people to get to where I am.

8. If you had the chance to start over again, would you do anything differently? More to the point, if you would, what's the reason?

I would get a PhD earlier. Good education is important and really helps.

I have no regrets in my life. I never did anything crazy. Didn't make bad decisions. Everything I have done have led to where I am at the moment. I have a loving husband and great children. I continue to nourish what I have. I am prepared to evolve into whatever is next.

There are always obstacles. Life is never easy. I just keep moving on even during low days. Things happen for a reason. There are phases in business and in life.

9. How would you characterize the state of Hispanic–Latino entrepreneurship in the United States? For instance, is it in the early stages, is it growing, or is it mature? Do you think it is open to all, or limited to certain individuals? Is it viable from anywhere in the country, or more favorable in certain states?

It's different across States. You see high levels of entrepreneurship in places like Miami and California. In Miami, I am impressed by how Cubans show their entrepreneurial qualities. They start all sorts of business. Some even start businesses right after they arrive in America. In California, you see a lot of food trucks operated by Latinos. In other States, we don't see as much entrepreneurship among Latinos. There's definitely room for growth. There are several model companies. Goya, for instance, became very successful in the country.

10. Are you a member of business organizations? Are these organizations unique to Hispanic–Latinos or open to all races? Did they contribute to your business success?

   I am a member of professional organizations in my field—i.e., dieticians. I am also a member of Hispanic organizations focused on business and leadership.

11. Do you think social networks and personal connections are important to business? Did you use networking when building your business, and are your social networks race based?

   Networking built my business. Everywhere you go, there are potential clients. Networking is huge specially if you are a consultant. It brings about business. People need to see you active, doing something, and getting things done.

12. If you could give advice to young Hispanic–Latino entrepreneurs or other young people thinking about starting a business, what would be the most important thing, and why?

   Have a vision. Yet, be prepared to change and evolve. Be savvy about money matters. Put money away and have some kind of financial cushion. Keep learning, never stop trying to grow.

   Have a passion for your chosen career. Pursue your passion, and money will follow. In my case, it's like a hunger that's never satisfied. I keep going at it and can't wait to get to work every day!

13. Have you been involved in sociocivic organizations or philanthropic work? If so, in which organizations, and what role did you play?

   I help out in several sociocivic and professional organizations. For instance, in public schools, church, Latino classes, promotion of healthy lifestyles, and the like. I even got involved in World Health Organization programs.

14. What do you see happening to your business in the future? Do you have succession plans in place? Do you see your business being run by family members or professional managers, and why?

I am at a cross-road in my business. One path could take me toward business expansion. It would mean hiring more people, and growing the business aggressively. Another path could be a partnership with a large company. It could also be a buy-out, a path toward retirement. I have not decided on the path yet. Whichever path I take, I would like to keep the passion for my work alive.

15. Where do you see yourself 10 years from now?

I want to be someplace warm and have many opportunities for travel. Retirement is still some time from now. I will have to balance my business growth and retirement decisions with family interests as well.

16. What do you think is your legacy to the business community?

My father passed away recently. He led a humble but meaningful life as Youth Director for the Seventh-day Adventist organization. He started a youth-oriented organization that encouraged outdoor activities in Latin America. He worked through limited resources, yet made an impact on the lives of many people. It was truly remarkable.

Thousands of people attended his funeral and paid his respects. People from all over the came to the funeral. It was quite touching.

I would like to leave a mark in a similar way. Ultimately, we will not be remembered for the money we made or the awards we've won. It's the people that we have touched who will remember us. How we'll be remembered will shape our legacy.

Many of us are blessed with so much resources. We have the ability to make a huge difference in this world.

Auto Shop Entrepreneur

Interview

1. Here we ask you to provide us an overview of your family history. For example, was there an entrepreneur in your family? Did your family history influence your decision to start a business?

My grandparents on my father's side of the family, along with my mother, were all entrepreneurs. My family history definitely influenced my decision to start my own business. They helped me realize that I did not want to work for someone. They reiterated the fact that I could make more money working for myself.

2. What was your educational background? Do you have specific views on formal versus informal education? What are your views on Hispanic–Latino entrepreneurial training programs? Has education contributed to your business success?

I went to Frankfort Community High School in Illinois. After high school, I studied automotive education at a technical school in Indianapolis. Frankfort is mostly a white community, and I was not treated differently from an education standpoint. I feel that Hispanic–Latino entrepreneurial training is on the rise. Education has contributed to my success from a business standpoint. At high school and at technical school, I did a lot of automotive work for classes.

3. Everyone has at least one role model, someone they aspire to be like. Do you have one who is an entrepreneur? How did they influence your decision to start a business?

My entrepreneurial role models are my grandparents. They started a business after my grandpa got out of the military. They also owned two pool halls and arcades. They now own a pawnshop.

4. Starting a new business isn't something people take lightly. Why did you start yours? What steps did you take to start the business?

I started my own business because I was sick of working for nickels and dimes on the dollar for other people. As an assistant manager at an automotive shop you only make $22,000 a year and that just isn't enough. I decided to go into detailing because in the past, I have done automotive accessories, performance parts, stereos, and I have always done work on cars. I started the detailing business because detailing cars is a passion for me. To start my business, I checked around for local competition to see what they were charging and the types of services they offered. I strived to make mine better.

5. What challenges did you face when building your business, and how did you overcome them? Did you come across any unique circumstances as a result of your race?

Frankfort has four other detailers with others in surrounding towns. To overcome all of this competition, I had to get my name out there so people knew I could do a better job than my competition. I did not come across any unique circumstances as a result of my race in Frankfort. I started my business in April this year. The first month, I made $1,500 then $2,200, then $4,000. I have been getting a lot of local business owners getting their cars detailed at my shop.

6. What types of support were most helpful to you when you were building your business? For example, did your local community play a role in shaping your business interests and development, or maybe it was a mentor? What or who was the one thing that made you believe, "Yes, I can do this!"

Since Frankfort is a small community that I grew up in, word of mouth traveled fast. I knew certain people and business owners in the community and everyone was helpful in aiding me to start my business. They wanted to see me succeed. People know that from my family history that my name was well respected and I just branched off my family's name. The respect that I got from the public was partially due to the encouragement I received from my mother and grandparents.

7. What do you think are the essential skills needed for Hispanic–Latino entrepreneurs to succeed in America? Also, what personal attitudes do you think are essential?

You really just need to be optimistic and open minded about what you can do. Don't let anybody hold you back. One county I lived in was quite racist and I grew up as one of the few Hispanics in town and felt negative vibes. The experiences in my youth made me think I couldn't do what I wanted to do. I'd like to stress that being optimistic is essential.

8. If you had the chance to start over again, would you do anything differently? More to the point, if you would, what's the reason?

With my business, I would have paid more attention where I spent my money. Especially through my website and certain products in my shop. Overall, I would not have done anything differently from a managerial standpoint. I offer things that nobody else offers. To be blunt, people want their cars cleaned and they don't want many options. I looked at my competitors that were offering discounts and always marketing things in their shops. I am able to compete because I am aware of what my competition offers.

9. How would you characterize the state of Hispanic–Latino entrepreneurship in the United States? For instance, is it in the early stages, is it growing, or is it mature? Do you think it is open to all, or limited to certain individuals? Is it viable from anywhere in the country, or more favorable in certain states?

   Hispanic entrepreneurship is growing in the United States and getting larger every day. I feel this is especially true in Illinois, a state that is mostly white. As time goes, it will keep growing just like anything else. I take blacks as an example, because there used to not be many black people who owned businesses and now there are numerous businesses that I can think of.

10. Are you a member of business organizations? Are these organizations unique to Hispanic–Latinos or open to all races? Did they contribute to your business success?

    No, I am not a member of any business organization so they did not contribute to my success in the automotive industry.

11. Do you think social networks and personal connections are important to business? Did you use networking when building your business, and are your social networks race based?

    Yes, social networks are very important. I use Twitter and Facebook to advertise everyday. My website doesn't do as good as Facebook because I had so many personal contacts on Facebook. This also allows me to get to know my customers on a more personal level which is big on the car community.

12. If you could give advice to young Hispanic–Latino entrepreneurs or other young people thinking about starting a business, what would be the most important thing, and why?

The best advice I can give is don't get discouraged if things don't go as planned the first time around. Rome wasn't built in a day. The most important thing is that starting a business is trial and error. You don't know what is out there until you try it.

13. Have you been involved in sociocivic organizations or philanthropic work? If so, in which organizations, and what role did you play?

Not particularly, every month I try to make some contribution to different organizations such as make a wish, relay for life, or breast cancer awareness.

14. What do you see happening to your business in the future? Do you have succession plans in place? Do you see your business being run by family members or professional managers, and why?

I see taking on one or two employees. I currently have well-known people in the community calling and asking for jobs, people older than me. I would like to have a couple of employees. My business is on track to make about $30,000 in its first eight months. My clients tend to want their vehicles detailed every couple of months. I see a 5 to 7 percent increase on the business end. I see my business being run by my family members, but I have a long way to go before that happens. I see this business growing into something great as long as I can keep offering great quality service.

15. Where do you see yourself 10 years from now?

Hopefully with the way things are going, set in multiple towns or having a business in a big town with a growing community where I can have trained employees and no longer have to do the work. I would love to have five to six trained employees working for me so it would be easier to expand the business.

16. What do you think is your legacy to the business community?

When it's all said and done, I want to be known as a respectful and trustworthy person who does good work. I want people to come to my shop and be known as more than a customer. I feel that customers deserve the fullest respect from employees.

Restaurant Owner 1

Interview

1. Here we ask you to provide us an overview of your family history. For example, was there an entrepreneur in your family? Did your family history influence your decision to start a business?

   Yes, my brother shaped my decision to start a business.

2. What was your educational background? Do you have specific views on formal versus informal education? What are your views on Hispanic–Latino entrepreneurial training programs? Has education contributed to your business success?

   I didn't finish high school. Not aware of any Hispanic–Latino programs. In my case, education did not contribute to my business success, work experience did.

3. Everyone has at least one role model, someone they aspire to be like. Do you have one who is an entrepreneur? How did they influence your decision to start a business?

   A friend served as a role model. I replicated the way he ran his business.

4. Starting a new business isn't something people take lightly. Why did you start yours? What steps did you take to start the business?

   I started my business because I had the courage to succeed. I had 20 years of work experience.

5. What challenges did you face when building your business, and how did you overcome them? Did you come across any unique circumstances as a result of your race?

   Financial challenges and lack of family support were challenges. I overcome them by working long hours. No, race was not an issue for me.

6. What types of support were most helpful to you when you were building your business? For example, did your local community play a role in shaping your business interests and development, or maybe

it was a mentor? What or who was the one thing that made you believe, "Yes, I can do this!"

I surrounded myself with professional people that I could trust.

7. What do you think are the essential skills needed for Hispanic–Latino entrepreneurs to succeed in America? Also, what personal attitudes do you think are essential?

Forge ahead—get a good support group. Don't let jealous people knock you down. Positive thinking and having a thick skin is essential.

8. If you had the chance to start over again, would you do anything differently? More to the point, if you would, what's the reason?

Nothing—nothing beats experience.

9. How would you characterize the state of Hispanic–Latino entrepreneurship in the United States? For instance, is it in the early stages, is it growing, or is it mature? Do you think it is open to all, or limited to certain individuals? Is it viable from anywhere in the country, or more favorable in certain states?

Hispanic entrepreneurship in the United States is growing. Now, it's available to everyone, everywhere.

10. Are you a member of any business organizations? Are these organizations unique to Hispanic–Latinos or open to all races? Did they contribute to your business success?

No, I am not a member of any business organization.

11. Do you think social networks and personal connections are important to business? Did you use networking when building your business, and are your social networks race based?

Yes, they are. But, I didn't use them much in building my business.

12. If you could give advice to young Hispanic–Latino entrepreneurs or other young people thinking about starting a business, what would be the most important thing, and why?

Get a strong support group. But more importantly have experience under your feet.

13. Have you been involved in sociocivic organizations or philanthropic work? If so, in which organizations, and what role did you play?

    No.

14. What do you see happening to your business in the future? Do you have succession plans in place? Do you see your business being run by family members or professional managers, and why?

    I plan on working until I die.

15. Where do you see yourself 10 years from now?

    Same place, only older.

16. What do you think is your legacy to the business community?

    That an uneducated minority can succeed. As long as you have the drive and experience. Don't jump in blindly.

Technology Entrepreneur

Interview

1. Here we ask you to provide us an overview of your family history. For example, was there an entrepreneur in your family? Did your family history influence your decision to start a business?

   No. I come from a humble family from Bogotá, Colombia. We couldn't afford a computer. Since I wanted a computer so badly, I had to figure out ways of making money in order to buy it. At the age of 14 I started offering data entry services. That was my first business.

2. What was your educational background? Do you have specific views on formal versus informal education? What are your views on Hispanic–Latino entrepreneurial training programs? Has education contributed to your business success?

I went to college to study Mechatronics. I dropped out at the end of second year as I was learning more on my business. I think that formal education is not very useful for entrepreneurs in certain industries, as technology. I'm not familiar with them—only a small fraction of it.

3. Everyone has at least one role model, someone they aspire to be like. Do you have one who is an entrepreneur? How did they influence your decision to start a business?

Elon Musk and Jeff Bezos. I try to imagine what they would do.

4. Starting a new business isn't something people take lightly. Why did you start yours? What steps did you take to start the business?

I've started 11 businesses. Each one is a different story. The first one was built out of necessity, as described on the first question. I figured a simple business model (data entry). I went to a bank and asked for the manager. The manager asked me for my pitch and I gave it to her. Given that I was 14 at the time, I think she ended up lending me personal money. I then posted bills all over my neighborhood letting people know we would do data entry for them. It worked! We had plenty of work. More than what we could handle.

5. What challenges did you face when building your business, and how did you overcome them? Did you come across any unique circumstances as a result of your race?

*Each business has had unique challenges. The list would be **very** long to write now! Yes. With my firm, we had a few haters that didn't like the idea of immigrants disrupting their industry.*

6. What types of support were most helpful to you when you were building your business? For example, did your local community play a role in shaping your business interests and development, or maybe it was a mentor? What or who was the one thing that made you believe, "Yes, I can do this!"

My wife's support. She is also a Latina. For my first business, I didn't think about it. I simply tried! For my firm, it was seeing the success of other Latino entrepreneurs in Miami.

7. What do you think are the essential skills needed for Hispanic–Latino entrepreneurs to succeed in America? Also, what personal attitudes do you think are essential?

It depends on the business. Each business requires different skills. The same as for non-Hispanics: passion, persistence, and being a bit crazy.

8. If you had the chance to start over again, would you do anything differently? More to the point, if you would, what's the reason?

I would be more confident of my skills. I would try to get more mentors earlier on. Being shy with my skills has reduced the risk sizes we had taken, which, in turn, has slowed down our growth. Mentors would have challenged some of my wrong ideas earlier on, thus saving time.

9. How would you characterize the state of Hispanic–Latino entrepreneurship in the United States? For instance, is it in the early stages, is it growing, or is it mature? Do you think it is open to all, or limited to certain individuals? Is it viable from anywhere in the country, or more favorable in certain states?

Unfortunately, I don't have enough info to properly answer this first question. I think it is open to all, but many Latinos don't feel like it. It may be easier to do it in areas with a dense Latino population, where it is easy to see other successful Latino entrepreneurs.

10. Are you a member of business organizations? Are these organizations unique to Hispanic–Latinos or open to all races? Did they contribute to your business success?

I'm member of Meetup, which are informal business organizations. Most of them are open to all. A few are focused on Latinos. Yes, both types.

11. Do you think social networks and personal connections are important to business? Did you use networking when building your business, and are your social networks race based?

Yes! Yes, and sometimes.

12. If you could give advice to young Hispanic–Latino entrepreneurs or other young people thinking about starting a business, what would be the most important thing, and why?

Only do it if you don't care about working 80 hours per week. The work is hard, but the rewards are great!

13. Have you been involved in sociocivic organizations or philanthropic work? If so, in which organizations, and what role did you play?

    Yes. BogoTech, founder; BogoDev, founder; ColombiaCare, advisor; EnseñaXColombia, advisor.

14. What do you see happening to your business in the future? Do you have succession plans in place? Do you see your business being run by family members or professional managers, and why?

    Growing and, most of them, being sold. Midterm, yes. Long term: Sell them. Professional managers. I don't like to work with family members as I've had bad experiences.

Social Enterprise Entrepreneur

Interview

1. Here we ask you to provide us an overview of your family history. For example, was there an entrepreneur in your family? Did your family history influence your decision to start a business?

    I grew up in a single family household. My father passed away from a heart attack at the age of 38 and my mother was diagnosed with breast cancer shortly after. While on chemotherapy, my mother's options narrowed a bit. She worked from home to support her three daughters. A few jobs included selling catalog products, natural herbs and teas, clothes, as well as babysitting from home. As a child, I soon began working odd jobs myself. I took my mother's shelf, painted it and called it "The Gift Shop." I made choker jewelry, Barbie and Cabbage patch clothes, sold stickers, mixed tapes, and perfumes. Soon it evolved into a pop-up shop in my elementary school during my lunch hour. This is where I hired my first assistant.

2. What was your educational background? Do you have specific views on formal versus informal education? What are your views on Hispanic–Latino entrepreneurial training programs? Has education contributed to your business success?

I received my bachelor of arts from the University at Buffalo in 2003 and studied abroad at the University of Havana in 2001. Courses such as marketing, interpersonal communication, advertising, public relations, and Spanish all help me with business decisions today. I immersed myself in many Latino/minority organizations such as PODER: Latinos Unidos, where I served on the executive board as the Secretary. Other memberships included LASA: Latin American Student Association and EOPSA, where I hosted a high school student for the weekend. I never took a Latino entrepreneurial training program, but am glad they are out there. Growing up in a drug-infested neighborhood, I wasn't around many role models. But with my mother's persistence, I went away to college. Being exposed to a college community was a culture shock. People actually wanted to study and better themselves. The people I met along with the experiences made greatly influenced my business success.

3. Everyone has at least one role model, someone they aspire to be like. Do you have one who is an entrepreneur? How did they influence your decision to start a business?

   In college I was lucky enough to have a mentor. She came into my life as part of an assignment and quickly became so much more. She supported my decisions and pushed me when I was ready to quit college. Even when I doubted myself, she never stopped believing. Her strength and ability to keep picking herself up during her darkest moments inspired me to keep moving forward.

4. Starting a new business isn't something people take lightly. Why did you start yours? What steps did you take to start the business?

   The disappointment of working long hours for someone and not being appreciated forced me to look beyond my situation. I was constantly drained and depressed. I had to make a change, so I made the decision of quitting my job of four years. Here's the tough part. I combined my savings, Individual Retirement Account (IRA) and a home equity to start my business. It was a risk I truly believed in.

5. What challenges did you face when building your business, and how did you overcome them? Did you come across any unique circumstances as a result of your race?

The biggest challenge has been hiring. The ability to trust that someone else will love this job as much as I do is difficult. In my field, we deal with live animals. We are liable for their safety. I run thorough criminal background checks, reference checks, and have my Pet Caregivers become Pet First Aid certified.

I do feel like I have to work harder to earn credibility because I am a young female with an accent. I think the first impression most people get is that they can get over on me.

6. What types of support were most helpful to you when you were building your business? For example, did your local community play a role in shaping your business interests and development, or maybe it was a mentor? What or who was the one thing that made you believe, "Yes, I can do this!"

I was surrounded by close friends who believed in my passion. At my previous job, I was physically sick with migraine headaches and terrible sinus infections. I told one of my friends I wanted to quit. She supported me all the way.

7. What do you think are the essential skills needed for Hispanic–Latino entrepreneurs to succeed in America? Also, what personal attitudes do you think are essential?

You need to have a can-do attitude with your clients; customer service is so important and is ultimately what leads to referrals. More importantly, self-discipline to wake up every morning even if it is to work from home. It can be so easy to get distracted with television, personal call, etc.

8. If you had the chance to start over again, would you do anything differently? More to the point, if you would, what's the reason?

The ability to clock out. I hope to be able to shut off my phone, laptop for a week, and have my business run without me having to check-in one day. Right now, we're still young and growing, so checking in is a necessity.

9. How would you characterize the state of Hispanic–Latino entrepreneurship in the United States? For instance, is it in the early stages, is it growing, or is it mature? Do you think it is open to all, or limited

to certain individuals? Is it viable from anywhere in the country, or more favorable in certain states?

I believe entrepreneurship is open to hard-working individuals who are willing to put in the time, money, and sweat before seeing substantial results. When you have your own business, you work more hours than you may ever have worked in an office because you never check out. You must be willing to sacrifice your social life for the first few years and have the finances to back you up.

10. Are you a member of business organizations? Are these organizations unique to Hispanic–Latinos or open to all races? Did they contribute to your business success?

Though none are Latino, I am a member of InGoodCompany, a shared office for women entrepreneurs; Crave NYC, an urban guide to female-owned businesses; PSI, Pet Sitters International; APSE, Association of Professional Sitting Excellence; NAPPS, National Association of Professional Pet Sitters. Although they may not have contributed to my success, these organizations are a great resource for discussions, continuing education, and a source of networking events. Presentation, publicity, and word of mouth are the biggest factors in increasing business.

11. Do you think social networks and personal connections are important to business? Did you use networking when building your business, and are your social networks race based?

Believe it or not my first clients were from Craigslist. Most of my networks are not race based. I go to networking events and mingle with the friendliest faces. The more they see my face at events the more they are likely to refer me.

12. If you could give advice to young Hispanic–Latino entrepreneurs or other young people thinking about starting a business, what would be the most important thing, and why?

Self-discipline. You should have the ability to work in an unstable environment and have the flexibility to change in order to consistently improve.

13. Have you been involved in sociocivic organizations or philanthropic work? If so, in which organizations, and what role did you play?

Every year we hold a pet food and linen drive to donate to several pet rescues such as: Animal Relief Fund, American Society for the Prevention of Cruelty to Animals (ASPCA), Growl Rescue, and the Animal Care and Control (AC&C). We also participate in the Relay for Life (cancer walk) and pet benefits for Stray from the Heart, Animal Haven, and more.

14. What do you see happening to your business in the future? Do you have succession plans in place? Do you see your business being run by family members or professional managers, and why?

    At the moment this is a one woman show. We are still growing and maturing. My sisters are professionals in their own fields, one being a Nurse Practitioner and Real Estate Investor and the other being a Guidance Counselor. I do have plans of partnering up with other professionals in my field in the near future. You can't do everything yourself, if you want to evolve.

15. Where do you see yourself 10 years from now?

    I see myself owning a stable business with newly developed departments, and in the stages of going national.

16. What do you think is your legacy to the business community?

    My business was conceived with the belief that every pet owner can make a difference. A portion of every dog walk, cat sit, and sleepover goes toward helping homeless pets have the opportunity to live with a family, outside of a cage. I hope to be a large factor in making this happen.

Beauty Industry Entrepreneur

Interview

1. Here we ask you to provide us an overview of your family history. For example, was there an entrepreneur in your family? Did your family history influence your decision to start a business?

    I was born in Greeley Colorado, a small town north of Denver. When I was 19, I took a big step and moved to NYC. My parents married when they were teenagers and migrated from Namiquipa Chihuahua, Mexico, to Colorado. The agricultural labor available in which they continuously labored to support my siblings and I was in high demand in Colorado at the time. I dreamed of getting out of that situation, as I spent many of my summers working in the fields as a young child and throughout my school years.

2. What was your educational background? Do you have specific views on formal versus informal education? What are your views on Hispanic–Latino entrepreneurial training programs? Has education contributed to your business success?

I have worked with various lucrative cosmetic lines in both sales and as a makeup artist. I noticed immediately the lack of product available for women of different ethnicities, especially Latin olive skin tones. I inquired for a position in product development within the companies I worked with and was informed that a college degree was required to obtain such a position.

When I was five my mother was already a single mother of five and Spanish was the only language spoken at home. Thus making school very challenging for me from the get go yet graduating high school was one of my first goals I had set myself and achieved. I can't say that education has contributed to the success of my business, on the contrary. The lack of education has made my journey a learning process in which all that I have experienced has made my journey a treasured one. However, an education would have helped me immensely and would have provided a less rocky road. Knowledge is power and I encourage all youth to continue no matter how hard and challenging it may be.

3. Everyone has at least one role model, someone they aspire to be like. Do you have one who is an entrepreneur? How did they influence your decision to start a business?

My role model is my mother. She has demonstrated so much strength, and has many creative talents. Had she been given the support or different circumstances in her life, she could have easily become a designer herself. She made all my clothes throughout my school years. To make extra money she utilized her incredible talent to create artificial flower arrangements, beaded jewelry, and all types of knitting, which she sold to friends and in yard sales. I remember her making a Spanish dancer's dress out of paper Mache, my older sister Trischa wore it in her talent show and was featured in our local Greeley Tribune. I get my creative inspiration from my mother.

4. Starting a new business isn't something people take lightly. Why did you start yours? What steps did you take to start the business?

   This is true! I never dreamt of starting my own business, but due to the inability to obtain a position in product development for any cosmetic line, I decided I would create my own position. However, where and how would I do this? It seemed completely impossible yet every day I did something toward learning how to create one. From 2000 through 2008 I gave myself a self-directed master class in manufacturing, design, and distribution in cosmetics.

   Being from a Latin background, we usually find ourselves without the guidance or resources to start the basics in life; such as, obtaining bank accounts, establishing or maintaining good credit, etc. I focused on establishing and fixing my credit and learned about financing. After I was approved for a small business loan in 2007, I knew it was my destiny to keep working toward my goal, as it now appeared to be attainable. In 2008, I launched my brand.

5. What challenges did you face when building your business, and how did you overcome them? Did you come across any unique circumstances as a result of your race?

   As mentioned before, not having a college education or knowing anything about starting a business, let alone running a business were two of my biggest challenges. However, research, research, and more research is an education in itself. Had I had the funds to start my business without doing so much research from 2000 through 2008, I believe I wouldn't be in business today. There is so much more that goes into starting a business besides the belief of having a great product. Baby step worked out best for me.

6. What types of support were most helpful to you when you were building your business? For example, did your local community play a role in shaping your business interests and development, or maybe

it was a mentor? What or who was the one thing that made you believe, "Yes, I can do this!"

I certainly didn't know how to put a business plan together, and one is needed to structure the vision of your business or to seek investors. So continuing my research in this category, I quickly became intimidated and discouraged. I felt hopeless and stuck. Without any finances to hire someone to help me, I came up with a clever thought of approaching, NYU, Pratt University, Harvard, and Columbia University to help. I had nothing to lose. Finding as many resources to do the things you can't is not impossible. Just go out and find them. To this day I am so grateful for the programs offered by such Universities. Columbia University students Amanda and Bassam were part of the team who put my initial plan together.

7. What do you think are the essential skills needed for Hispanic–Latino entrepreneurs to succeed in America? Also, what personal attitudes do you think are essential?

First and foremost, believe you can do anything you set your mind to! Your passion will guide you. Think positive as you will always encounter discouragement and many obstacles, but do not let it take over and never give up.

8. If you had the chance to start over again, would you do anything differently? More to the point, if you would, what's the reason?

I wouldn't change a thing. It's almost like saying "I wish I knew then, what I know now." It's the experience that has put me where I am now. Shoulda, coulda, woulda, doesn't matter at this point. If I were no longer in business, then I could say there would be many things I would change. But for now, I am exactly where I envisioned myself.

9. How would you characterize the state of Hispanic–Latino entrepreneurship in the United States? For instance, is it in the early stages, is it growing, or is it mature? Do you think it is open to all, or limited to certain individuals? Is it viable from anywhere in the country, or more favorable in certain states?

It's definitely in the growing stage. You can start your business from anywhere, and at anytime. Research is at our fingertips, realizing that technology provides us the resources to succeed and is unlimited. (Internet, social media, etc.) Sky is the limit!!

10. Are you a member of business organizations? Are these organizations unique to Hispanic–Latinos or open to all races? Did they contribute to your business success?

Currently I am a certified business within the NYNJMSDC, New York & New Jersey Minority Supplier Development Council; WEBE, Women's Business Enterprise National Council, which are both nonprofit organizations to support minority and women business owners. Also, CEW (Cosmetic Executive Women) a trade beauty industry organization which provide support and networking for tomorrow's leaders in the industry. These organizations haven't contributed to my success, however, being a member with them has sure helped me network and could potential have an influence on my business.

11. Do you think social networks and personal connections are important to business? Did you use networking when building your business, and are your social networks race based?

I believe it is a good to get yourself out there. I still haven't mastered building my business through social media networks. However, I hope to utilize and use social networks as an outreach source to share my documentary on how I started my business along with keeping my clients updated with the latest products or news regarding my cosmetic line. I also love using YouTube, I post tutorials on how to use my products, etc., which are instrumental and effective.

12. If you could give advice to young Hispanic–Latino entrepreneurs or other young people thinking about starting a business, what would be the most important thing, and why?

*Have a plan. Envision yourself accomplishing your goal, do your research, and master each and every step during your learning process. **Never** throw in the towel. You can do it!!*

13. Have you been involved in sociocivic organizations or philanthropic work? If so, in which organizations, and what role did you play?

Yes, I wish I could do more but for now I donate products to the women at the Women's Shelter of Domestic Violence in NYC, and have donated products for charity events for organizations such the Happy Faces Foundation, affiliated with the Ronald McDonald House who houses families with children battling cancer, Dream Project which helps build the resources to education children in the Dominic Republic, and Orphaned Starfish Foundation. I look forward to becoming more involved as a Philanthropist.

14. What do you see happening to your business in the future? Do you have succession plans in place? Do you see your business being run by family members or professional managers, and why?

    I wear all the hats in my business and have worked alone until I hired my advisory team in 2013. Getting the right team together as you grow makes all the difference. I look forward to running my business for the next 5 to 10 years and building a great exit strategy which would allow me to continue to be the chief creative director, as it is my goal to become a top innovative leader in the beauty industry.

15. Where do you see yourself 10 years from now?

    *In ten years, my brand **will be** recognized as one of the top innovative leaders in luxury products such as handbags, jewelry, cosmetics etc. and a household name.*

16. What do you think is your legacy to the business community?

    My legacy is my passion and determination to inspire women and young kids in achieving their dreams, and becoming their own superhero to the next generation.

Motorsports Consultant

Interview

1. Here we ask you to provide us an overview of your family history. For example, was there an entrepreneur in your family? Did your family history influence your decision to start a business?

My dad is a doctor and my mom is an artist. I wouldn't necessarily describe my family as entrepreneurial, but they have definitely always stressed that you have to work hard and be honest. As far as my family goes, the way they helped me become an entrepreneur was by always supporting me in whatever I decided to do and never pressing me to go the "traditional" route of business.

2. What was your educational background? Do you have specific views on formal versus informal education? What are your views on Hispanic–Latino entrepreneurial training programs? Has education contributed to your business success?

I grew up in Mexico and went to elementary school in Mexico City; then high school in Austin, Texas; and finally I got a BS in advertising from the University of Texas at Austin. Although college was a great experience and it helped give me some basics into the world of marketing and PR, in reality, most of my experience and training has come from actually on the job training, reading, and simply from absorbing as much as possible from my colleagues and bosses.

Although I do believe it's important to have a formal education, except for a few specific cases, I think it only serves as a base to get to know your industry and to start to learn how to network. What makes you grow as a person and as an entrepreneur is what you learn outside of school, most of the times is what can't really be thought specifically but can be absorbed from being around experts. Life is about knowing how to interpret situations, understanding relationships and behaviors, managing expectations, and being so immersed in your field that no matter what comes up you have the mental and business resources to deal with it.

3. Everyone has at least one role model, someone they aspire to be like. Do you have one who is an entrepreneur? How did they influence your decision to start a business?

I've never had one specific role model that I've followed and have aspired to be like, but I have had a variety of different mentors and supporters that have taught me different skills and ways of doing business, and navigating in the business world. Different people from my boss, to my client, to my roommate, everybody always has something to offer and is better than you at something, I try to absorb as much as possible from any person that I'm close to.

4. Starting a new business isn't something people take lightly. Why did you start yours? What steps did you take to start the business?

I've always had a passion for motorsports, and after working directly both with drivers and teams, I noticed an opportunity to fill a gap. There was an important untapped market specifically dealing with Hispanic drivers, and Hispanic motorsport marketing and I saw the opportunity with my experience and connections to be one of the firsts to take advantage of it.

5. What challenges did you face when building your business, and how did you overcome them? Did you come across any unique circumstances as a result of your race?

Staying afloat during a recession. Motorsports is a luxury and it was severely hit by the economy, and being a start up at that time made it very difficult. But making it through also created many opportunities, as a lot of the competition did not survive. My race actually opened up opportunities because there is always a demand for Hispanic marketing and PR in motorsports, the only problem has been that in some ways I have been stereotyped as being able to focus exclusively in Hispanic related projects, when in reality a significant part of my business focuses on general market.

6. What types of support were most helpful to you when you were building your business? For example, did your local community play a role in shaping your business interests and development, or maybe it was a mentor? What or who was the one thing that made you believe, "Yes, I can do this!"

The first time I realized that I really could do this was when my first client, a race car driver, decided to hire me and put his trust in me. Although I had experience, it had always been from working for somebody else, this was the first time that I was going to go on my own, with no support, and he believed in me. Having him as a client gave me not only the experience but also the reputation and prestige to grow my business and slowly acquire new clients. We are now close friends.

7. What do you think are the essential skills needed for Hispanic–Latino entrepreneurs to succeed in America? Also, what personal attitudes do you think are essential?

In my case being Hispanic has given me a lot of opportunities because with our community growing so much in America, the need for business people that can relate in a culturally relevant way to the Hispanic market is bigger by the day. You need to understand how your skills and background differ from others and how to turn these differences into advantages over your competition. You must be proactive and always try to stay a step ahead of the rest, and in my case, at least, honesty is an extremely important attitude.

8. If you had the chance to start over again, would you do anything differently? More to the point, if you would, what's the reason?

I'm happy with the opportunities that I've taken advantage of and wouldn't really change much. Obviously, if you look back, you can always improve, but that's not how life works. The only thing I would do different, and it's something that I'm trying to do currently, is be more organized in better training the people that work for me so they can take on more responsibilities, and in turn allow me to focus more on big picture items.

9. How would you characterize the state of Hispanic–Latino entrepreneurship in the United States? For instance, is it in the early stages, is it growing, or is it mature? Do you think it is open to all, or limited to certain individuals? Is it viable from anywhere in the country, or more favorable in certain states?

I believe it is growing, and it is at a very attractive point in its growth, with the latest census numbers. The huge influence that Latinos have in the United States in every aspect of life is now very clear. As far as business goes, most companies are beginning to realize that they must cater to this market more intensely, and they will be looking for people and companies that can take over these responsibilities. This will open up many opportunities for Hispanic entrepreneurs to quickly grow their businesses. The next few years will be very exciting, then it will eventually settle back down to normal business. This is an important time to take advantage of our cultural background and take advantage of opportunities before somebody else does.

10. Are you a member of business organizations? Are these organizations unique to Hispanic–Latinos or open to all races? Did they contribute to your business success?

    Yes, I am a member of MexNet Alliance which is a nonprofit group that focuses on providing free small business education to Latinos in Central Texas. They provide seminars in Spanish on the basics of how to start, maintain, and grow a small business.

    Although, I became a part of their board of directors after I started my business; they have served as an inspiration and have taught me that no matter what kind of skills or experience you have, you can always find a way to give back to the community. Also being involved with his organization has been a great networking tool for my business.

11. Do you think social networks and personal connections are important to business? Did you use networking when building your business, and are your social networks race based?

    Yes, absolutely. I believe that in this day and age this is one of the most important aspects in my business. Not only do we use social network as a means of generating revenue and as our primary marketing and promotional tool for our clients, it is also the main tool that we use for self-promotion and to create a company image.

    I use social media more and more every day, and although I'm very involved with it, its constantly evolving and you have to work hard to keep up and be on the cutting edge of this phenomenon.

    Our social networks combine different languages, and it is always a challenge that we are still learning how to best deal with properly.

12. If you could give advice to young Hispanic–Latino entrepreneurs or other young people thinking about starting a business, what would be the most important thing, and why?

You need to have a lot of patience and never lose sight of your long-term goals, even when the odds are against you, you need to stay focused and get through the hard times. Realistically things don't happen overnight, and you will have a lot more failures than successes, but you have to keep planting seeds and preparing yourself, because eventually the opportunity that you have been waiting for will come by and you need to be able to not only recognize it, but take advantage of it. Being an entrepreneur is not only about coming up with new ideas, no matter how unique or innovative your concepts are, if you don't sacrifice and work hard, they will never become a reality.

13. Have you been involved in sociocivic organizations or philanthropic work? If so, in which organizations, and what role did you play?

I am the cofounder of Racing for Mexico which is an organization that utilizes motorsports to reach the Hispanic community and develops programs that allow fans and sponsors to help the community in many different ways.
   I was also the director of communications for a sociocivic firm.

14. What do you see happening to your business in the future? Do you have succession plans in place? Do you see your business being run by family members or professional managers, and why?

I see it spreading over many different areas of the motorsports industry, and taking on a much bigger role based around Hispanic marketing. I do not have plans in place, and I would never want it to be run completely by somebody else. I would however like to step back and focus on big ticket items only while others handle the day to day operations.

15. Where do you see yourself 10 years from now?

I see myself as a top influencer and leader of the industry, with a family, and enough experience and success to be able to pick and choose what I spend my time on.

16. What do you think is your legacy to the business community?

I hope that people will realize that I'm doing something that nobody else has done properly, which is to combine a variety of services that are needed in the motorsports marketing industry. And by focusing primarily in the Hispanic market aspects of the sport, I am creating a must-have suite of services for anybody that is looking to succeed, whether it is a driver, a team, or a sponsor.

Web Entrepreneur

Interview

1. Here we ask you to provide us an overview of your family history. For example, was there an entrepreneur in your family? Did your family history influence your decision to start a business?

Around the time I was 11 years old my aunt bought her first restaurant, and I wanted to one day have my own restaurant like my aunt. My step-father also had his own gardening business. I like how they were able to work on their own and how they were able to hire awesome co-workers.

2. What was your educational background? Do you have specific views on formal versus informal education? What are your views on Hispanic–Latino entrepreneurial training programs? Has education contributed to your business success?

Right after graduating from San Marcos High School, I wasn't sure if I wanted to continue school. A friend convinced me to take a night bookkeeping class at the local city college. After that class, I started to go full time. After one too many years at Santa Barbara City College, I transferred to Westmont College. After only one year at Westmont College, I transferred and graduated from University of California Santa Barbara (UCSB).

I believe having formal education is beneficial to all who can flourish in it. I know there are some people that tend to do much better having informal education.

Having the structured learning in high school and college, I was able to learn many subjects and meet great teachers and students. I personally feel that getting any sort of informal education is great. I see this as thinking out of the circle. Getting trained by people or learning from people not at a structured setting would enhance someone's perspective. For instance, while going to high school I learned variable subjects.

When I was around 11 years old I got my own paper route, and learned from it. Having my own paper route taught me at a young age the value of work and money. I wasn't good at saving money, but I learned that in order to buy items that I wanted like Nintendo Games, you have to work at it.

I believe that Hispanic–Latino entrepreneurial training programs need to be created because a majority of us live through the same family experiences and can relate to each other. Also, the training programs would be great to help Latinos collaborate and possibly create something like the next top electronic product, or Children Tech centers, or the next Facebook.

Education has contributed to my business learning and success. I also think that going out in the world and talking to other entrepreneurs has played a big role in my business success. Talking to experts or basically people that have been successful is key. To listen and learn is paramount. For example, going to networking events with other entrepreneurs is fun, but if you do not listen and learn from other entrepreneurs, you're not helping yourself.

3. Everyone has at least one role model, someone they aspire to be like. Do you have one who is an entrepreneur? How did they influence your decision to start a business?

   Growing up, I had the chance to see a few entrepreneurs. In high school, two entrepreneurs I loved reading about were Henry Ford and Bill Gates. Both of these men had ideas that changed their industries and the world. Seeing how both men influenced their industries motivated me to start to think and create a business in the future.

4. Starting a new business isn't something people take lightly. Why did you start yours? What steps did you take to start the business?

I started my firm because I was motivated while attending the Pubcon Conference in Las Vegas. After seeing countless people in tech talk about Entrepreneurship and Twitter, it motivated me to start my firm, a directory of Twitter users. After the conference I started to write down notes and asked a number of people what they would like in a Twitter directory. After doing extensive research, I also started to research for a name and began the design of the website.

5. What challenges did you face when building your business, and how did you overcome them? Did you come across any unique circumstances as a result of your race?

A couple of challenges I faced when building the business was the lack of other entrepreneurs in my city (Santa Barbara). Luckily, I was able to travel to Los Angeles, Las Vegas, and San Francisco to a many thriving tech networking conferences.

It was a little hard going to my first conference. I did not know anyone and I tried to look for other Latinos that could relate to me. At the tech conferences, there were a few Latinos. At my first conference, I met an awesome person. Emily probably saw me looking lost and she introduced herself to me, and we proceeded to walk together meeting people. Wow. She was a life-saver. After my first conference experience, I gained confidence and was able to start conversations with people I did not know. After attending many tech conferences, I would see that the Latino community needs to be better represented.

6. What types of support were most helpful to you when you were building your business? For example, did your local community play a role in shaping your business interests and development, or maybe it was a mentor? What or who was the one thing that made you believe, "Yes, I can do this!"

The most helpful support I received when I started my firm was the other people I met at the conferences. Also, Santa Barbara started to have a local tech/Twitter scene. There were fantastic local Search Engine Optimization (SEO) workshops with Taylor Reaume, a Santa Barbara startup group with Mike Lewis, and the Santa Barbara Tweetup group.

Having these local community events helped me tremendously with shaping my development of my firm and my other business.

When people started tweeting me or expressing their love of my firm's concept in person, it motivated me to keep expanding and continue creating other websites.

7. What do you think are the essential skills needed for Hispanic–Latino entrepreneurs to succeed in America? Also, what personal attitudes do you think are essential?

To succeed in America as a Hispanic–Latino entrepreneur, one has to push oneself to keep going. Keep going and creating. Never doubt yourself and listen and learn. As an entrepreneur either having a website or restaurant or any kind of business, one must be ready to take criticism of your product. Listen and analyze all constructive criticism you get. At times it helps to receive feedback from other people.

8. If you had the chance to start over again, would you do anything differently? More to the point, if you would, what's the reason?

If I had a chance to start over again, I would have started my website creating at a younger age and kept creating while I was at UCSB. In college, I stopped creating and just focused on college. While I was very busy in college, I should have reserved more time to being an entrepreneur.

9. How would you characterize the state of Hispanic–Latino entrepreneurship in the United States? For instance, is it in the early stages, is it growing, or is it mature? Do you think it is open to all, or limited to certain individuals? Is it viable from anywhere in the country, or more favorable in certain states?

I believe the state of Hispanic–Latino entrepreneurship in the United States is growing in certain areas. I would like it to grow faster in the technology sector. It's open to anyone who has an idea to create, or has the motivation to do something fun and different. It is viable in any area of the country, but being close to metropolitan areas is most advantages for networking and promoting.

10. Are you a member of business organizations? Are these organizations unique to Hispanic–Latinos or open to all races? Did they contribute to your business success?

Currently, I'm not a member of any business organization.

11. Do you think social networks and personal connections are important to business? Did you use networking when building your business, and are your social networks race based?

I do believe that social networks and personal connections are important to any business. Many times entrepreneurs get their product or themselves noticed via the social networks. I used a lot of networking when building my business. My social networks are not race based. In today's social network scene, all races are represented in the social networks.

12. If you could give advice to young Hispanic–Latino entrepreneurs or other young people thinking about starting a business, what would be the most important thing, and why?

The most important thing I would tell young Hispanic–Latino entrepreneurs or any entrepreneur is to start now. Do not wait. Start your idea and don't be hesitant with your idea. If you don't have an idea but the thought of entrepreneurship interests you, go to some startup Meetups or conferences. And more importantly listen and learn.

13. Have you been involved in sociocivic organizations or philanthropic work? If so, in which organizations, and what role did you play?

I have not been involved in philanthropic work.

14. What do you see happening to your business in the future? Do you have succession plans in place? Do you see your business being run by family members or professional managers, and why?

In the future, I would like to see my business be more successful and popular. If I moved on to other things, I would try to give the site to another aspiring entrepreneur who is willing to take my website to a higher level. I do see myself creating more online businesses in the future, and just maybe try a restaurant or two with my lovely wife who has been the reason for my success.

15. Where do you see yourself 10 years from now?

    I would like to see myself still creating fun and unique businesses and phone applications. I would also like to try having a restaurant.

16. What do you think is your legacy to the business community?

    My legacy to the business community would be how I was able to create unique and fun businesses for people to use.

Real Estate Entrepreneur

Interview

1. Here we ask you to provide us an overview of your family history. For example, was there an entrepreneur in your family? Did your family history influence your decision to start a business?

   Yes, my father has a small factory of cosmetic products (shampoo, body lotion, etc.). He always encouraged me not to be an employee, but have my own company. My mother is a psychologist, she works on her own as well.

2. What was your educational background? Do you have specific views on formal versus informal education? What are your views on Hispanic–Latino entrepreneurial training programs? Has education contributed to your business success?

   I have a bachelor's degree in human resources. Universities in Argentina don't prepare people for starting a business; they prepare people to work in multinationals companies.

3. Everyone has at least one role model, someone they aspire to be like. Do you have one who is an entrepreneur? How did they influence your decision to start a business?

   My father is my role model. Andy Freire (founder of Officenet) was a good inspiration for me. He wrote a great book: Pasion por emprender.

4. Starting a new business isn't something people take lightly. Why did you start yours? What steps did you take to start the business?

Four things: I always wanted to have my own business, I wanted to work with foreigners, I love to connect people with what they are looking for, and my last boss decided I didn't serve him anymore. I saw there was a problem with foreigners trying to find a room in my city, so I decided to create a company that helped them. I didn't think too much at first, I've just worked and worked.

5. What challenges did you face when building your business, and how did you overcome them? Did you come across any unique circumstances as a result of your race?

    Renting a room in Buenos Aires is a very new habit, so I needed to create confidence in people. I needed to explain people what was all this about.

6. What types of support were most helpful to you when you were building your business? For example, did your local community play a role in shaping your business interests and development, or maybe it was a mentor? What or who was the one thing that made you believe, "Yes, I can do this!"

    My family and friends helped me a lot, they encouraged me to continue. One year after I founded my firm and set bit up in Buenos Aires. I entered the bid challenge, and they assigned me a great mentor that helped a lot with my company! I didn't win the competition, but my mentor was great!

7. What do you think are the essential skills needed for Hispanic–Latino entrepreneurs to succeed in America? Also, what personal attitudes do you think are essential?

    You need to be prepared to see the opportunity and the right moment. You need to be persistent. You need to trust in your idea and you need to be clever and flexible to adapt to changes. In America, nothing is like what books say. You need to make your own way.

8. If you had the chance to start over again, would you do anything differently? More to the point, if you would, what's the reason?

    I'd be more risky; sometimes, I am too afraid to succeed and I don't take too many risks.

9. How would you characterize the state of Hispanic–Latino entrepreneurship in the United States? For instance, is it in the early stages, is it growing, or is it mature? Do you think it is open to all, or limited to certain individuals? Is it viable from anywhere in the country, or more favorable in certain states?

I don't know this, I am sorry.

10. Are you a member of business organizations? Are these organizations unique to Hispanic–Latinos or open to all races? Did they contribute to your business success?

I am a member of Unión Argentina de Jóvenes Empresarios (entrepreneurship young members) and Enablis. All are open to all races.

11. Do you think social networks and personal connections are important to business? Did you use networking when building your business, and are your social networks race based?

Yes, absolutely! When I started my company I went to all the events I could; I deliver my business card to everyone! Networking is a must!

12. If you could give advice to young Hispanic–Latino entrepreneurs or other young people thinking about starting a business, what would be the most important thing, and why?

To believe in you and in your idea. To find the niche and start!

13. Have you been involved in sociocivic organizations or philanthropic work? If so, in which organizations, and what role did you play?

Not yet, but I have a good project in mind!

14. What do you see happening to your business in the future? Do you have succession plans in place? Do you see your business being run by family members or professional managers, and why?

It's a difficult question for me since I am going to become a mother in a few weeks. At least I want to continue working and try to expand my business.

15. Where do you see yourself 10 years from now?

Love to have a company, maybe something with products, but definitely be my own boss.

16. What do you think is your legacy to the business community?

Impact on people, helping people. I want to keep long business relationships (my father taught me that), and I want to be a good business person.

Fast Food Industry Operator

Interview

1. Here we ask you to provide us an overview of your family history. For example, was there an entrepreneur in your family? Did your family history influence your decision to start a business?

Yes, a family member, specifically, my brother influenced me to start a business. I saw my brother succeed and thought that if he could do it, so could I.

2. What was your educational background? Do you have specific views on formal versus informal education? What are your views on Hispanic–Latino entrepreneurial training programs? Has education contributed to your business success?

I attended some college. I believe it is better to go to school. However, if you can't complete your college education go as far in college as you can, and then go ahead and start the business, because you can be successful without a college education. I am unaware of any Hispanic–Latino entrepreneurial training programs. I do not feel that my education contributed to my success. I believe that most Hispanics do not need an education to start or be successful in a business in the United States.

3. Everyone has at least one role model, someone they aspire to be like. Do you have one who is an entrepreneur? How did they influence your decision to start a business?

I looked up to chain businesses, such as Subway and Papa Johns, as a business model to aspire for and model myself after.

4. Starting a new business isn't something people take lightly. Why did you start yours? What steps did you take to start the business?

I aspired to start my own business because I was tired of working for somebody else. I wanted to be able to send my children to college for a better life. I wanted to provide a better life for my children. I started with a grocery store. My brother had a truck and was successful, so I thought I could be successful too.

5. What challenges did you face when building your business, and how did you overcome them? Did you come across any unique circumstances as a result of your race?

The language barrier was a problem. I found it difficult to find the right resources. I knew that they existed, but it was difficult to ascertain information due to the language barrier.

6. What types of support were most helpful to you when you were building your business? For example, did your local community play a role in shaping your business interests and development, or maybe it was a mentor? What or who was the one thing that made you believe, "Yes, I can do this!"

My brother is the only one that played a role in my starting a business. I saw that my brother was successful in his mobile restaurant. I figured that if he could be successful, so could I.

7. What do you think are the essential skills needed for Hispanic–Latino entrepreneurs to succeed in America? Also, what personal attitudes do you think are essential?

Language is essential. It was a barrier for me. I believe you must have the right information as to how to start a business. It would be great if there were classes offered on how to start a business. It would make things easier for many entrepreneurs. With regard to the personal attitude, it was a strong desire to succeed that helped me be successful.

8. If you had the chance to start over again, would you do anything differently? More to the point, if you would, what's the reason?

I wouldn't do anything differently if I had a chance to start over again. I believe I have learned along the way and am doing good business now.

9. How would you characterize the state of Hispanic–Latino entrepreneurship in the United States? For instance, is it in the early stages, is it growing, or is it mature? Do you think it is open to all, or limited to certain individuals? Is it viable from anywhere in the country, or more favorable in certain states?

I believe the state of Hispanic–Latino entrepreneurship is in its growing stages. Anyone can be successful in any state in the United States if you have the skill. In the case of the food industry—food is everywhere, so you can succeed anywhere.

10. Are you a member of business organizations? Are these organizations unique to Hispanic–Latinos or open to all races? Did they contribute to your business success?

No, I am not a member of any business organization.

11. Do you think social networks and personal connections are important to business? Did you use networking when building your business, and are your social networks race based?

Social networks and personal connections are important in starting and building a business. However, one should focus strictly on business. It is best not to hire relatives, and just hire from the community. It prevents conflict. My social network is not race-based, although all my employees are Latino.

12. If you could give advice to young Hispanic–Latino entrepreneurs or other young people thinking about starting a business, what would be the most important thing, and why?

Save money prior to starting a business, as you will need plenty of capital. Also, go to school. If unable to finish school, start a business anyway, as you will be successful without the schooling, but the schooling will be helpful.

13. Have you been involved in sociocivic organizations or philanthropic work? If so, in which organizations, and what role did you play?

No, I have not been involved in sociocivic organizations or philanthropic work. I would like to be involved in such activities. But right now, I am quite busy growing the business.

14. What do you see happening to your business in the future? Do you have succession plans in place? Do you see your business being run by family members or professional managers, and why?

I am planning on expanding my business in the next 10 years with more trucks. I am also planning on moving to Florida with a fleet of trucks. Ultimately, I will franchise my operations. I want my children to go to college to have the advantages that a college education offers and to be able to choose what they want to do with their lives.

15. Where do you see yourself 10 years from now?

In Florida, taking a rest. I see myself with a chain business or with a fleet of trucks. I want to start the chain business but am unsure of the procedures, and the way to make this happen. I need more information on how to accomplish my goals. I believe, if I had the necessary information on how to accomplish this goal, I would be successful at it. I do not know where to go to get accurate and necessary information on how to achieve this goal. I need to know who can help me accomplish this goal on a large scale.

16. What do you think is your legacy to the business community?

People can taste real Mexican food from my trucks. I believe most Americans don't know what real Mexican food tastes like. Most Mexican food in America don't have the flavors and ingredients that my food does. That's why I want to introduce my product here. Most people say they will try one taco, then they come back and want four or five because of the ingredients. They love the quality of the ingredients and the taste. I want to show American consumers what real Mexican food tastes like.

Car Dealership Operator

Interview

1. Here we ask you to provide us an overview of your family history. For example, was there an entrepreneur in your family? Did your family history influence your decision to start a business?

Nobody in my family was an entrepreneur before me. I came up with a decision to start a business by myself.

2. What was your educational background? Do you have specific views on formal versus informal education? What are your views on Hispanic–Latino entrepreneurial training programs? Has education contributed to your business success?

Formal education can be beneficial tool, but it needs to be accompanied by hard work and experience. As far as Hispanic–Latino entrepreneurial training programs, I never knew they existed. They sound like they could be helpful for some people. Education has not contributed to my success, life experiences have.

3. Everyone has at least one role model, someone they aspire to be like. Do you have one who is an entrepreneur? How did they influence your decision to start a business?

My role model is Jorge Vergara. Jorge Vergara is a Mexican man who started very small and continuously worked his way up the ladder. Now he is huge and worth billions. He is the founder of Grupo Omnilife, which is one of the top 200 corporations in Mexico. He also owns Chivas (a soccer club) and real estate. I heard him speak one time and found his story inspirational.

4. Starting a new business isn't something people take lightly. Why did you start yours? What steps did you take to start the business?

I started my business for many reasons. The most important being that I wanted to create a legacy for my children. I started small, buying and selling cars on the street, and slowly the business got bigger. From there, I got a business license, purchased a property, and started slowly building inventory and selling it.

5. What challenges did you face when building your business, and how did you overcome them? Did you come across any unique circumstances as a result of your race?

Challenges I faced when starting my business were the poor economy, government regulation, and taxes are high in the used car sales business.

It is also a poor economy so it makes it hard because a lot of people do not have the money to purchase groceries, let alone a car. Nothing unique happened because I am Hispanic.

6. What types of support were most helpful to you when you were building your business? For example, did your local community play a role in shaping your business interests and development, or maybe it was a mentor? What or who was the one thing that made you believe, "Yes, I can do this!"

My wife was most helpful to me while building my business. My family provided excellent support. My used car sales business is mainly family operated.

7. What do you think are the essential skills needed for Hispanic–Latino entrepreneurs to succeed in America? Also, what personal attitudes do you think are essential?

The most essential skills needed for Hispanic–Latino entrepreneurs who want to succeed in America are: they need to speak English, be persistent, give good customer service, and have a good work ethic. The attitude that is very essential is a positive personal attitude.

8. If you had the chance to start over again, would you do anything differently? More to the point, if you would, what's the reason?

I would have waited until Obama was out of office because the economy might be better. The current economic environment and unemployment rate has a negative impact on my business.

9. How would you characterize the state of Hispanic–Latino entrepreneurship in the United States? For instance, is it in the early stages, is it growing, or is it mature? Do you think it is open to all, or limited to certain individuals? Is it viable from anywhere in the country, or more favorable in certain states?

Hispanic–Latino entrepreneurship is rapidly growing. Business is open to all and not limited to certain individuals. I don't know much about other states, but you can do business anywhere if you had a great idea.

10. Are you a member of business organizations? Are these organizations unique to Hispanic–Latinos or open to all races? Did they contribute to your business success?

I am not a member of any business organization.

11. Do you think social networks and personal connections are important to business? Did you use networking when building your business, and are your social networks race based?

Absolutely, social networks and personal connections are very important to creating a prosperous business. I receive a lot of referrals from family and friends. Good customer service and referrals from customers who have had good customer experiences help my business. My social network is somewhat race-based since a lot of my friends are Hispanic.

12. If you could give advice to young Hispanic–Latino entrepreneurs or other young people thinking about starting a business, what would be the most important thing, and why?

My advice to young Hispanic–Latino entrepreneurs and young entrepreneurs in general is give excellent and equal customer service to everyone and your business will flourish. Customer service is the most important thing in your business, because happy customers bring other happy customers.

13. Have you been involved in sociocivic organizations or philanthropic work? If so, in which organizations, and what role did you play?

No.

14. What do you see happening to your business in the future? Do you have succession plans in place? Do you see your business being run by family members or professional managers, and why?

In the future, I hope that we get more capitalist-minded leadership in the country in order to grow this business and become more successful. I would like to expand my business enough to get another location. Currently, I do not have a succession plan in place. I see the business being run by family-members as well as professional managers. This combination would be the key to future success.

15. Where do you see yourself 10 years from now?

I see myself growing the business by having a second location.

16. What do you think is your legacy to the business community?

My legacy to the business community would be hopefully to provide added strength to business leadership in the community

Auto Repair and Detailing Entrepreneur

Interview

1. Here we ask you to provide us an overview of your family history. For example, was there an entrepreneur in your family? Did your family history influence your decision to start a business?

My cousins are owners of a chain of Mexican restaurants in Monticello, Illinois and in California. I knew that I wanted to be an entrepreneur, but not in the food industry. They had an influence on this decision to become a business owner but not necessarily in the field that I got into.

2. What was your educational background? Do you have specific views on formal versus informal education? What are your views on Hispanic–Latino entrepreneurial training programs? Has education contributed to your business success?

I did not finish high school because I was forced to start working a full-time job at age 16. I was able to obtain my certificate in auto body repair later without a formal high school diploma. Formal education is important, but in my case it did not affect me because I learned most of my skills from my uncle who is also an auto body repair mechanist. I also taught myself a lot of things, which led to my success. I am not familiar with any specific entrepreneurial training programs in the area. This program would be very positive for Hispanic–Latinos in the community.

3. Everyone has at least one role model, someone they aspire to be like. Do you have one who is an entrepreneur? How did they influence your decision to start a business?

My role model is my uncle, who owns and works at an auto body shop in California. He also has taught me everything since I was 13. My uncle encouraged me to start my own business in Decatur.

4. Starting a new business isn't something people take lightly. Why did you start yours? What steps did you take to start the business?

It was hard for me to obtain a job being a Hispanic. My business is the only thing I do well and enjoy. I had all of the tools, and got a permit, to start my business and found a building to do my work in Decatur. I didn't do much in the way of advertising. I mainly did work by word of mouth and, also, went to people's houses and repaired their cars, before I built my customer base.

5. What challenges did you face when building your business, and how did you overcome them? Did you come across any unique circumstances as a result of your race?

The challenges that I faced when building my business were getting customers to give me a chance. I started to do a little advertising and made it clear that my prices were cheaper than my competitors. I also got a lot of business by word of mouth from the few people that I knew in the area. I had a hard time getting people to trust that I did good quality work because of my race. This discouraged me at times.

6. What types of support were most helpful to you when you were building your business? For example, did your local community play a role in shaping your business interests and development, or maybe it was a mentor? What or who was the one thing that made you believe, "Yes, I can do this!"

My brother lives in Decatur, as well, and he helped me not get discouraged. I took his advice to advertise more even if it would cost more than I would have liked to spend. Also, seeing my cousins in Monticello build their restaurant business gave me motivation that I could accomplish my goals and succeed at my own business.

7. What do you think are the essential skills needed for Hispanic–Latino entrepreneurs to succeed in America? Also, what personal attitudes do you think are essential?

The most essential skill for success in America is definitely knowing English and being able to interact with people. Also, getting advice from Americans and watching how they do business is a good idea, as well. Also, education is more important to Americans, which means staying in school and getting a high school diploma is becoming essential.

8. If you had the chance to start over again, would you do anything differently? More to the point, if you would, what's the reason?

If I had to do things differently, I would try to focus on doing business for dealerships rather than work for individuals. Although, I see this as a possible opportunity in the future. I already established a reputation for doing "cheap work" with good quality.

9. How would you characterize the state of Hispanic–Latino entrepreneurship in the United States? For instance, is it in the early stages, is it growing, or is it mature? Do you think it is open to all, or limited to certain individuals? Is it viable from anywhere in the country, or more favorable in certain states?

Hispanic Latino entrepreneurship is still growing in the United States. There are a lot of Mexican restaurants but there are still plenty of opportunities for more businesses operated and owned by Hispanics. Having an education gives people an advantage over those who do not, which could limit certain individuals. American expectations for education in certain fields are higher compared to those who are Hispanic.

10. Are you a member of business organizations? Are these organizations unique to Hispanic–Latinos or open to all races? Did they contribute to your business success?

I am a member of The Voice of Small Businesses. This organization helps protect my rights as a small business owner. I am currently not a member of any Hispanic–Latino organizations but have been thinking about joining Laraza Legal Rights, which helps fights for equal rights for Hispanics.

11. Do you think social networks and personal connections are important to business? Did you use networking when building your business, and are your social networks race based?

Social networks help enhance my image and get me more business. I currently don't have a Facebook page for my business but am thinking about starting one. Personal connections are the primary way I get business. I have loyal customers that come back multiple times and also refer more people to me. I use networking such as word of mouth to start my business but now use yellow pages, wheels and deals, and an established website.

12. If you could give advice to young Hispanic–Latino entrepreneurs or other young people thinking about starting a business, what would be the most important thing, and why?

    I would advise Hispanic–Latinos to stay in school and also learn from Americans. Never be shy to ask for help or advice because that is the key to success. Also, like mentioned earlier in the interview, getting the proper education is becoming more and more essential even though I didn't go down that path.

13. Have you been involved in sociocivic organizations or philanthropic work? If so, in which organizations, and what role did you play?

    No.

14. What do you see happening to your business in the future? Do you have succession plans in place? Do you see your business being run by family members or professional managers, and why?

    I would like to expand my business to more locations. I already started on this plan by contacting auto body shops in Peoria, Illinois. The only issue I am facing is getting workers for this location. I would like to have family members work at this other location but not very many of them have the same skills set.

15. Where do you see yourself 10 years from now?

    I would like to have multiple locations while still residing in Decatur, Illinois.

16. What do you think is your legacy to the business community?

    My legacy to the business community would be to consistently lend support to individuals and dealerships on their automobile needs.

Restaurant and Food Service Owner

Interview

1. Here we ask you to provide us an overview of your family history. For example, was there an entrepreneur in your family? Did your family history influence your decision to start a business?

   Yes, my brother was an entrepreneur, but no one in my family influenced my decision to start my own business.

2. What was your educational background? Do you have specific views on formal versus informal education? What are your views on Hispanic–Latino entrepreneurial training programs? Has education contributed to your business success?

   I went to school until junior high school. I do not believe that formal or informal education matters; we do not have a formal education, and we still have a successful business. Education has not really contributed to my success as I only have a junior high school education. The only thing that matters is that you are dedicated to be successful.

3. Everyone has at least one role model, someone they aspire to be like. Do you have one who is an entrepreneur? How did they influence your decision to start a business?

   I do not have a role model, but my parents always worked hard and that inspired me to never give up.

4. Starting a new business isn't something people take lightly. Why did you start yours? What steps did you take to start the business?

   I started my business because it was a unique opportunity, and a risk that I was willing to take. I worked multiple other jobs until we saved up enough money to take the chance on our own business.

5. What challenges did you face when building your business, and how did you overcome them? Did you come across any unique circumstances as a result of your race?

   The most challenging problem we have faced is probably the economy. We are just doing everything in our power to not give up.

6. What types of support were most helpful to you when you were building your business? For example, did your local community play a role in shaping your business interests and development, or maybe it was a mentor? What or who was the one thing that made you believe, "Yes, I can do this!"

   The greatest support came from my family. The thing that motivated me the most was the feeling of owning your own business. I believed owning my own business would be a great feeling.

7. What do you think are the essential skills needed for Hispanic–Latino entrepreneurs to succeed in America? Also, what personal attitudes do you think are essential?

   Hispanic–Latino entrepreneurs need to be bilingual, always have a positive attitude, and never give up on what you want to accomplish.

8. If you had the chance to start over again, would you do anything differently? More to the point, if you would, what's the reason?

   In hindsight, I would choose not to have partners. In not having partners, we would avoid disagreements.

9. How would you characterize the state of Hispanic–Latino entrepreneurship in the United States? For instance, is it in the early stages, is it growing, or is it mature? Do you think it is open to all, or limited to certain individuals? Is it viable from anywhere in the country, or more favorable in certain states?

   The state of the Hispanic–Latino entrepreneurship in the United States is slowly growing. I believe that it could be open to all but it depends on the individual trying to get into it than it does on the Hispanic–Latino entrepreneurial community keeping them out.

10. Are you a member of business organizations? Are these organizations unique to Hispanic–Latinos or open to all races? Did they contribute to your business success?

No, I do not belong to any business organization and I have not heard of any.

11. Do you think social networks and personal connections are important to business? Did you use networking when building your business, and are your social networks race based?

    Social networks and personal connections are important to business. Yes, I do use social networking to help build my business. We currently have a Facebook account.

12. If you could give advice to young Hispanic–Latino entrepreneurs or other young people thinking about starting a business, what would be the most important thing, and why?

    Do not give up, always fight for your business. Dedication is key in completing anything.

13. Have you been involved in sociocivic organizations or philanthropic work? If so, in which organizations, and what role did you play?

    No.

14. What do you see happening to your business in the future? Do you have succession plans in place? Do you see your business being run by family members or professional managers, and why?

    I want the business to grow, continue to grow, while keeping the same values and culture we have. The business will continue to be run by family.

15. Where do you see yourself 10 years from now?

    Traveling and opening up more chains of restaurants.

16. What do you think is your legacy to the business community?

    The importance of being polite to customers and how it affects the publicity the restaurant gets.

Landscaping and Gardening Service Entrepreneur

Interview

1. Here we ask you to provide us an overview of your family history. For example, was there an entrepreneur in your family? Did your family history influence your decision to start a business?

   The only other entrepreneur in the family was my cousin. He had a huge influence on my starting my landscaping business since he already had his own up and running.

2. What was your educational background? Do you have specific views on formal versus informal education? What are your views on Hispanic–Latino entrepreneurial training programs? Has education contributed to your business success?

   I had very little education background. I was done with school around the age of 11 since I had work and other responsibilities around my home. I was taught to read and write at a very young age by a female teacher under a tree so I got a very informal education growing up.

   I never received any form of training. Education was not a factor in my success.

3. Everyone has at least one role model, someone they aspire to be like. Do you have one who is an entrepreneur? How did they influence your decision to start a business?

   The one person I really looked up to was my older brother, Aubel. I wanted to be just like him. However, I also looked up to my cousin as a role model. Especially, since it was my cousin who showed me the ropes.

4. Starting a new business isn't something people take lightly. Why did you start yours? What steps did you take to start the business?

   I started my business because I was basically tired of working long hours and having little money to show for it. I worked as a welder for about 17 years and also cleaned offices at night.

   First, I went with my cousin to work and really liked what he did. So I worked with my cousin for a few weeks. There were days that I worked from

6 AM to 7 PM. People really liked my individual work, so the owners of the house I was doing landscaping for would ask me to come back. The owners would recommend me to other people around the neighborhood. So after I saved up a little bit of money, I bought a little truck and quit my welding job. I continued to clean offices until I had more clients. Soon after, I had more yard routes, and I quit my office cleaning job and just did yard routes.

5. What challenges did you face when building your business, and how did you overcome them? Did you come across any unique circumstances as a result of your race?

   The hardest challenge I faced was learning the English language. So I went back to school for a very short time just to learn how to speak the language. I never had any complications due to my race.

6. What types of support were most helpful to you when you were building your business? For example, did your local community play a role in shaping your business interests and development, or maybe it was a mentor? What or who was the one thing that made you believe, "Yes, I can do this!"

   My community had a huge role in my business, developing into what it is today. I started off with very few clients, but with hard work I was able to impress the few I had and they would spread the word about my work. I was my own motivator. I wanted to make more money, and do something I enjoyed doing.

7. What do you think are the essential skills needed for Hispanic–Latino entrepreneurs to succeed in America? Also, what personal attitudes do you think are essential?

   The most essential skill to be successful in America as a Hispanic entrepreneur and achieve the "American dream" is to learn the language, the more you know the better.

   The most important attitudes are: hard work, dedication, discipline, and punctuality.

8. If you had the chance to start over again, would you do anything differently? More to the point, if you would, what's the reason?

I would do everything the exact same way. I was fortunate to start learning the business from a family member.

9. How would you characterize the state of Hispanic-Latino entrepreneurship in the United States? For instance, is it in the early stages, is it growing, or is it mature? Do you think it is open to all, or limited to certain individuals? Is it viable from anywhere in the country, or more favorable in certain states?

It is in the early stages, and very difficult for Hispanic entrepreneurs due to the language and culture barriers.

It's open to people who are willing to put in the time to learn the English language.

With regard to the different states, success depends on the type of business the Hispanic–Latino entrepreneur is trying to start in reference to its viability. Clearly, there are more Hispanics and Latinos in States like California, Florida, and big cities like Chicago.

10. Are you a member of business organizations? Are these organizations unique to Hispanic–Latinos or open to all races? Did they contribute to your business success?

No ties to any business organization.

11. Do you think social networks and personal connections are important to business? Did you use networking when building your business, and are your social networks race based?

Yes, they are. But, since I had little education, I never got involved in social networking.

12. If you could give advice to young Hispanic–Latino entrepreneurs or other young people thinking about starting a business, what would be the most important thing, and why?

You should be kind to others, be honest, and most importantly learn the English language.

13. Have you been involved in sociocivic organizations or philanthropic work? If so, in which organizations, and what role did you play?

I do philanthropy work through my church but other than that nothing else.

14. What do you see happening to your business in the future? Do you have succession plans in place? Do you see your business being run by family members or professional managers, and why?

    In four to five years, I want to sell my business preferably to someone in the family. I would like to be able to sell it but yet earn a percentage of profit off the business. I would like to keep it in the family because it's important for me to always help family out when you can.

15. Where do you see yourself 10 years from now?

    I see myself buying and flipping houses 10 years from now. There is really good money in the area where I live.

16. What do you think is your legacy to the business community?

    I would like to be remembered by my business community as a hard-working and honest man who worked well with others.

Organizational Entrepreneur or Intrapreneur

Interview

1. Here we ask you to provide us an overview of your family history. For example, was there an entrepreneur in your family? Did your family history influence your decision to start a business?

    Most from father's side were Cubans who came to America and worked hard to be their own boss. My father owns business, and friends do as well. For the past four years, I have been working at a restaurant which started out as a small carry out food business and now is a really successful Cuban Café, and this has inspired me to grow and learn from my experiences.

2. What was your educational background? Do you have specific views on formal versus informal education? What are your views on Hispanic–Latino entrepreneurial training programs? Has education contributed to your business success?

I originally had started off at a university and did not know what major I wanted to have, but now that I know what direction I want to go, and that is management. Formal background is the key to success, but I think informal background is just as important because you have to have a prominent social impact to the community in order to succeed.

3. Everyone has at least one role model, someone they aspire to be like. Do you have one who is an entrepreneur? How did they influence your decision to start a business?

   My father and close friends were my role models. My main role model is my boss who started a restaurant from ground up and now is a multimillion dollar company. With his help, I was able to learn how to run the restaurant.

4. Starting a new business isn't something people take lightly. Why did you start yours? What steps did you take to start the business?

   The steps that are needed to be taken first pertain to getting an education. To have a successful operation, you have to show people what you have done. You always have to be fascinated with what you do, and be able to have your own establishment.

5. What challenges did you face when building your business, and how did you overcome them? Did you come across any unique circumstances as a result of your race?

   Consistency is the biggest challenge in any business. You have to be able to provide the same customer service night in and night out, so always being consistent is key, and I think people respond to Latino culture well.

6. What types of support were most helpful to you when you were building your business? For example, did your local community play a role in shaping your business interests and development, or maybe it was a mentor? What or who was the one thing that made you believe, "Yes, I can do this!"

   My biggest support is my boss. He helped me shape the standards of knowing what it takes to be successful.

7. What do you think are the essential skills needed for Hispanic–Latino entrepreneurs to succeed in America? Also, what personal attitudes do you think are essential?

Dedication and discipline is key; being able to dedicate your life to what you want do is something not everybody can accomplish. In the United States, there are so many opportunities to succeed.

8. If you had the chance to start over again, would you do anything differently? More to the point, if you would, what's the reason?

I would not change too much, from when I finished high school. I would have wanted to sit down and actually think about what I want to do; but other than that, I would not change anything.

9. How would you characterize the state of Hispanic–Latino entrepreneurship in the United States? For instance, is it in the early stages, is it growing, or is it mature? Do you think it is open to all, or limited to certain individuals? Is it viable from anywhere in the country, or more favorable in certain states?

I think it is viable anywhere. It is definitely in its growing stage and in about 10 to 20 years it will be maturing. Latino owners and business owners will be growing constantly over the years. It is viable just about anywhere, and, especially in America, the possibilities are endless.

10. Are you a member of business organizations? Are these organizations unique to Hispanic–Latinos or open to all races? Did they contribute to your business success?

Being part of a restaurant organization is definitely beneficial.

11. Do you think social networks and personal connections are important to business? Did you use networking when building your business, and are your social networks race based?

With technology today, the possibilities expand more than ever before. Having business cards and developing good relationships with people early and over the years is definitely important, because you never know when you are going to need somebody's help.

12. If you could give advice to young Hispanic–Latino entrepreneurs or other young people thinking about starting a business, what would be the most important thing, and why?

The most important thing to have is patience. Never rush into anything, take your time to learn the industry, and soak up the information that would make you successful.

13. Have you been involved in sociocivic organizations or philan-thropic work? If so, in which organizations, and what role did you play?

I have not done a lot of time in the community service aspect because I have been focusing most of my time on the restaurant. But, once I have everything established, I will contribute more time toward community service.

14. What do you see happening to your business in the future? Do you have succession plans in place? Do you see your business being run by family members or professional managers, and why?

I need to have professional managers because having family working for you is never a good idea. I want someone that is experienced. I am meet-ing with investors in May and presenting them my business plan for a social enterprise for young people in the Chicago area.

15. Where do you see yourself 10 years from now?

I see myself established in my business and having people recognize my business nationwide. I want to have the income to have my business running. And, most importantly, generate revenue to help young people nationwide.

16. What do you think is your legacy to the business community?

I want to leave a legacy as being the first generation Cuban American to graduate from college. I want to be able to enrich the community and have the community benefited from what I have done, and I want people to learn and grow from my accomplishments.

Restaurant Owner 2

Interview

1. Here we ask you to provide us an overview of your family history. For example, was there an entrepreneur in your family? Did your family history influence your decision to start a business?

   No, I was one of the first to start a business. I had a family to take care of. I didn't want to be stuck being a waiter. I was looking for a better future.

2. What was your educational background? Do you have specific views on formal versus informal education? What are your views on Hispanic–Latino entrepreneurial training programs? Has education contributed to your business success?

   High-school dropout. Dropped out when I was a junior in Mexico. No, I do not. I do not know much about them. School and real life are two very different things.

3. Everyone has at least one role model, someone they aspire to be like. Do you have one who is an entrepreneur? How did they influence your decision to start a business?

   No not really. I have surpassed all the ones I looked up to. I didn't.

4. Starting a new business isn't something people take lightly. Why did you start yours? What steps did you take to start the business?

   Because I didn't want to keep making money for someone else. I wanted to become my own owner. First dishwasher, cook, head cook, waiter, manager, then owner—a 10-year process.

5. What challenges did you face when building your business, and how did you overcome them? Did you come across any unique circumstances as a result of your race?

   I can't recall any challenges when I began but I know I ran into a lot. Overcoming them is very difficult, you have to be patient. Have the urge to keep moving forward and have heart.

6. What types of support were most helpful to you when you were building your business? For example, did your local community play a role in shaping your business interests and development, or maybe it was a mentor? What or who was the one thing that made you believe, "Yes, I can do this!"

My wife was the one that helped a lot; especially, saving money. My community had nothing to do with it. My family was all the support I had.

7. What do you think are the essential skills needed for Hispanic–Latino entrepreneurs to succeed in America? Also, what personal attitudes do you think are essential?

Skills are not needed. I had no experience when I started. All I had was my heart, family, and body. You have to give it your all, be good with people, be humble, and respect others and your job.

8. If you had the chance to start over again, would you do anything differently? More to the point, if you would, what's the reason?

No, I would keep everything the same.

9. How would you characterize the state of Hispanic–Latino entrepreneurship in the United States? For instance, is it in the early stages, is it growing, or is it mature? Do you think it is open to all, or limited to certain individuals? Is it viable from anywhere in the country, or more favorable in certain states?

I think it is growing, and it is open to all. It is viable anywhere in the country.

10. Are you a member of business organizations? Are these organizations unique to Hispanic–Latinos or open to all races? Did they contribute to your business success?

No, I am not. I don't know.

11. Do you think social networks and personal connections are important to business? Did you use networking when building your business, and are your social networks race based?

Yes. First of all free advertising. No, I did not.

12. If you could give advice to young Hispanic–Latino entrepreneurs or other young people thinking about starting a business, what would be the most important thing, and why?

Be responsible, and work hard.

13. Have you been involved in sociocivic organizations or philanthropic work? If so, in which organizations, and what role did you play?

No

14. What do you see happening to your business in the future? Do you have succession plans in place? Do you see your business being run by family members or professional managers, and why?

We'll hopefully expand one day if we keep up the good and hard work. Professional managers or just myself, why because I don't know if my kids like the idea, but I hope that one of them would.

15. Where do you see yourself 10 years from now?

I don't know. I live the present, I am not promised tomorrow.

16. What do you think is your legacy to the business community?

"No response provided"

Trucking and Concrete Business Owner

Interview

1. Here we ask you to provide us an overview of your family history. For example, was there an entrepreneur in your family? Did your family history influence your decision to start a business?

My grandfather had a farm he cultivated. The most popular thing he grew and sold very well was the Pitaya, a fruit that only blossoms and is popular in the month of May. I come from a very poor family. My father did not go to school therefore my grandfather cut him out financially. It was hard growing up not having much, and seeing other family members well off and have no desire to help. My father worked for my grandfather and so did I, but he did not give us much. He gave us the bare minimum to get by in life. My grandfather had no sympathy for his son or grandchildren.

2. What was your educational background? Do you have specific views on formal versus informal education? What are your views on Hispanic–Latino entrepreneurial training programs? Has education contributed to your business success?

I followed my father's footsteps and did not graduate high school. I believe education is very important, but I also believe desire, will, and being street smart can get you very far. I believe Hispanic–Latino entrepreneurial training programs are vital because programs like those can guide you, give you a path to follow, and show you what to do and how to get things done effectively. Without school or training, you are basically on an empty trail trying to find your way and just experimenting. You have to try everything to see what works and what does not work. My limited education has contributed to my success; the fundamentals I learned in middle school and high school in mathematics have been vital, as well as reading and writing. My children who have gone further in education have also helped me a lot.

3. Everyone has at least one role model, someone they aspire to be like. Do you have one who is an entrepreneur? How did they influence your decision to start a business?

My former boss, Bill. He believed in me and I loved working for him. He knew what to do, how to handle his business and personal life at the same time. He gave great advice and was a great teacher. He taught me how to negotiate and analyze a prospective job to give a price that would make me a winner. Due to the economic crisis, Bill had to lay me off (I was one of the highest paid workers). This was the best thing that happened to me. After laying me off, Bill pushed me to start my own business. He said I was ready and I would be a fool to go off and find a job in another company.

4. Starting a new business isn't something people take lightly. Why did you start yours? What steps did you take to start the business?

I started mine because I got laid off. I bought the equipment required in my business field: a tractor, 10 wheeler, shovels, etc. I then called people I knew and told them I was going off on my own to start my business.

I sold myself and I told them what I could do. People would tell me of potential customers and I eventually made calls and gave my business cards out.

5. What challenges did you face when building your business, and how did you overcome them? Did you come across any unique circumstances as a result of your race?

Language barriers. To converse with people I did business with at first was hard, but the more practice I got the more confident I became. The language barrier was part of my race.

6. What types of support were most helpful to you when you were building your business? For example, did your local community play a role in shaping your business interests and development, or maybe it was a mentor? What or who was the one thing that made you believe, "Yes, I can do this!"

Bill and my family. They inspired me and gave me motivation. I learned from other people who had their own business. They gave me great advice and also told me where to head to find clients.

7. What do you think are the essential skills needed for Hispanic–Latino entrepreneurs to succeed in America? Also, what personal attitudes do you think are essential?
Language domination as well as verbal and written skills. People need to be friendly, courteous, and have a strong desire and will to get ahead in life.

8. If you had the chance to start over again, would you do anything differently? More to the point, if you would, what's the reason?

I would plan things more effectively and efficiently. At first, I bought the required material but then I did not know the next step. I would have a game plan, seek training, and maybe take some business classes.

9. How would you characterize the state of Hispanic–Latino entrepreneurship in the United States? For instance, is it in the early stages, is it growing, or is it mature? Do you think it is open to all, or limited to certain individuals? Is it viable from anywhere in the country, or more favorable in certain states?

I believe it is growing, but it has not quite matured. I know many who start their business in the fields of construction or landscaping who are school dropouts and still need a few pointers. I believe it is open to all, anyone and everyone who has a dream, passion for something, and determination. I do not know about other areas. I hear Chicago and Texas are good, but I would say California is a very decent place for Hispanics.

10. Are you a member of any business organizations? Are these organizations unique to Hispanic–Latinos or open to all races? Did they contribute to your business success?

    No.

11. Do you think social networks and personal connections are important to business? Did you use networking when building your business, and are your social networks race based?

    I think they are very useful, but I feel they are more orientated toward bigger and stronger businesses. I did use a network, and I advertised my business on a radio show within my Hispanic community.

12. If you could give advice to young Hispanic–Latino entrepreneurs or other young people thinking about starting a business, what would be the most important thing, and why?

    Layout what you want to do and how you will get there. Design your path. It is better to have a plan than to go at it without having a clue. By taking some classes or having some sort of training will get you ready.

13. Have you been involved in sociocivic organizations or philanthropic work? If so, in which organizations, and what role did you play?

    No.

14. What do you see happening to your business in the future? Do you have succession plans in place? Do you see your business being run by family members or professional managers, and why?

    I see one of my sons taking it over. With their education, the business will become bigger and more successful. Because of my family and their professions, they will become professionals in the business and will know what the business needs in order to grow.

15. Where do you see yourself 10 years from now?

    Retired and living in Mexico.

16. What do you think is your legacy to the business community?

    I believe I am an inspiration to others and motivation to some. The community is able to see how I evolved. I started with nothing and now have something. I was able to create my business for myself and others. Whatever the environment may be, I am able to perform efficiently and effectively if I set my mind to it. I show that anything is possible.

CHAPTER 4

Conclusion

This book project was an interesting journey for the authors. Like all unforgettable journeys, there were unexpected twists and turns. There were moments of joy and moments of sadness. There were moments where we felt victorious, and in some instances we felt defeated.

Nevertheless, our journey may be valuable to many. The interviews we gathered framed the thinking of Hispanic–Latino entrepreneurs across America in the early part of the New Millennium.

While we did not obtain responses from a broader demographic segment of Hispanic–Latino entrepreneurs, the viewpoints shared by them were highly insightful. We believe the findings are relevant to the academic and business communities, as well as the general public. Government officials, international organizations, and think tanks can use some of the featured information to develop policies and programs.

In showcasing our findings, we feature the question asked and common responses. We will then proceed to discuss the business implications using an assessment paragraph.

Listed as follows are our findings.

Question	Responses
Role of family in entrepreneurial decision	• The push to become an entrepreneur was a desire to provide for the family. • Not one entrepreneur in the family so far. Consequently, no family member served as an entrepreneurial role model. • Family did not think it was a lucrative way to make money. • Females were not considered business professionals or entrepreneurs; so, starting a business was not encouraged. • The entrepreneur was motivated to become better off financially than parents. • Family owns their own business and inspired the entrepreneur to as well through dedication and perseverance. • Siblings all had the desire to create their own businesses and follow their passions.

Survey Assessment

The role of family in the entrepreneur's decision was quite varied. While some individuals wanted to provide for their families, others strived to match and surpass the level of success their parents had achieved through their entrepreneurial businesses. The level of support the entrepreneur received from the family often depended on their culture and traditions. For example, several female entrepreneurs received little to no support from their parents because it was believed that women were supposed to take care of the home and children rather than pursue personal business ventures. Other entrepreneurs received a great amount of support from their families in every step of the way, offering emotional, educational, and sometimes financial support along the way. With numerous family members starting their own businesses, the entrepreneurial spirit was simply in the blood of some entrepreneurs. From the role of family in the entrepreneurial decision, there was one common thread for the motivation of each entrepreneur, to be successful and continue to achieve their personal and professional goals.

Question	Responses
Role of education in business success	• Education is required in the field to remain competitive and up-to-date on the latest trends. • Informal education played just as integral a role in entrepreneurial success as formal education. • Real world experiences and hardships have taught the entrepreneur the most. • High school and college education provided the building blocks and basic business knowledge. • Professional and industry accreditations led to more customers. • Dropped out of high school or college. • Determination, motivation, and hard work are all you need to succeed. • Hispanic–Latino entrepreneurial training programs provide the necessary education and encourage personal growth. • Family taught the entrepreneur value business and life lessons that helped lead to success. • *Street smarts* can go a long way in the business environment. • Formal education broadens the mind and encourages the entrepreneur to grow.

Survey Assessment

Education played a key role in establishing a successful business for a majority of the entrepreneurs. Depending on the field or industry, higher education and accreditation may be required to expand the customer base, such as for nutrition experts, or to remain competitive in the industry. Many believe that obtaining a certain level of formal education allows the entrepreneur to get a foot in the door of a business opportunity. It provides the basic tools in which to create a successful and sustainable business. Entrepreneurial and business training sessions, especially Hispanic–Latino entrepreneurial programs, provided valuable advice and information. It allowed business owners to remove roadblocks and overcome challenges they faced while growing their businesses. Other entrepreneurs believe that informal education or *street smarts* can be just as valuable, or even more so, because the lessons go beyond the textbook in real life challenges and inequalities business owners face. Several entrepreneurs stress that motivation, the will to succeed and striving to be better will open doors and provide opportunities that would otherwise be difficult to accomplish.

Question	Responses
Who served as the role model?	• Not many role models desired to achieve the same goals as the entrepreneur. • Oprah Winfrey • Mother Teresa • Parents have inspired them to take risks and follow their dreams. • College mentor with never-ending support • Henry Ford • Bill Gates • Steve Jobs • Andy Freire • Regular individuals who can turn an idea into a successful venture. • Former boss or co-worker

Survey Assessment

Almost every entrepreneur had at least one role model that he or she used as a guide along the path to success. Some individuals had specific role

models while others had a group or an ideal, such as business professionals who desired to change the world and those who are never discouraged
when faced with set-backs. Role models and leaders were chosen for a variety of reasons. Many of the entrepreneurs have never met their career or
personal role models but have researched or observed enough about them
to understand their journey and philosophy. Oprah Winfrey and Mother
Teresa were chosen based on their kindness toward others and what they
could accomplish through peace, understanding, and support. Bill Gates
and Henry Ford offered the determination to change the industry and
innovative thinking that several entrepreneurs inspire toward. Several
of the inspirations for entrepreneurs were not entrepreneurs themselves
but led successful lives. Many entrepreneurs hold their parents, grandparents, and family members in high regard and hope to live up to what
they accomplished. The family members provided unwavering support
through tough times, continuously offered ideas for improvement, and
made the entrepreneurs think on their toes and learn from their past mistakes. Role models, in general, offer a life-story, attitude, belief, achievement, or status that others aspire to obtain, learn from, or go beyond.

Question	Responses
What were the drivers and steps for the business start-up?	• Laid off and let people know of business start-up • Asked others for potential customers. • Wanted to be the boss and set own work hours. • Sold items out of a truck or home to build a solid reputation and then expanded from there. • Purchased an existing business and the business model and perfected it. • Worked multiple jobs and saved up to take the opportunity. • Wanted to earn money for oneself rather than for some-one else. • Desired a flexible work schedule and to be home with the children more. • Saved up money to attend classes and receive accredita-tions in the industry. • Desired the freedom to develop personal ideas. • Began business as a partnership and parted ways to pursue personal opportunities. • Began with an idea that grew into a plan and a large network of business professionals.

Survey Assessment

Although profits and a high return often attract individuals to start their own businesses, these entrepreneurs chose their path for a variety of reasons. The power of being one's own boss and the flexible work hours it promises appealed to several entrepreneurs. Others desired to place their ideas and dreams into motion themselves while earning a larger salary. While some entrepreneurs were motivated to pursue their own passions, others became self-sufficient out of necessity, having been laid off from their current place of employment. With the decision to pursue a business the entrepreneurs began taking steps to expand their ideas into successful businesses online and speaking with friends and business professionals. Several individuals started a joint venture or enhanced a company already in business. Despite the differences, the common thread and one of the first steps in developing their businesses was to accumulate funds. The extra start-up resources came from retirement accounts, savings, multiple jobs, and interested parties of the entrepreneur. The entrepreneurs were willing to risk hard earned money and resources on their ventures in the hopes that the financial and personal return would be substantial.

Question	Responses
Challenges faced when starting the business	• Single mother in a male centered Hispanic family • Consistency in products and customer service from day to day. • Building a clientele of loyal consumers. • Communicating effectively with language barriers. • Race had little to no effect for entrepreneur. • Building a brand based on American standards. • Bridging the gap between blue collar and white collar businesses. • Marketing the company to target customers. • Trying to thrive despite the economy. • Finding the perfect location. • Overcoming gender roles and stereotypes. • Balancing work and family. • Receiving payments in a timely manner.

Survey Assessment

Starting a business is no easy task. Each entrepreneur faced a multitude of hurdles on his or her path to success. Several entrepreneurs experienced difficulty in marketing their product or service to their respective target markets. Even though the businesses offered high-quality products, many consumers were focused on the price and on popular brands. By focusing on key markets and providing strong customer service, the entrepreneurs built a robust list of loyal clientele. A major issue for many entrepreneurs was overcoming gender roles and stereotypes that forced them to prove their expertise on a higher level. Many of the entrepreneurs found the work-and-family mix difficult to balance, often having to spend long and late hours building their businesses instead of spending quality time with family. Surprisingly, the main issue related to race was overcoming the language barrier to establish effective communication with business professionals, customers, and industry partners.

Question	Responses
Who provided support when building the business?	• Networking with business professionals. • Family members were always there, cheering them on. • Fellow business owners who provided strong advice. • Friends provided encouragement through tough times. • Coaches offered motivation and will power to succeed. • Community raised awareness. • Workshops and seminars • Self-motivation • Spouse

Survey Assessment

Although every entrepreneur showed strong motivation to become successful and overcome challenges, each received support in the beginning stages of owning a business. The main support line came from family members who not only offered encouragement but also expertise and an extra set of hands when the work became overwhelming. Similar to family members, friends provided a support line and continued to push the entrepreneur to new levels. Other individuals relied on self-motivation to build their businesses. Creating extensive networks with business professionals provided several individuals with a strong foundation and led to future partnerships. Entrepreneurial workshops and seminars offered insightful and industry specific tips and advice that strengthened the entrepreneur's business plan and operations.

Question	Responses
Essential skills and attitudes needed for business success in America	• Dedication and discipline • Understand and be able to speak the language • Take advantage of all the opportunities • Have the mindset to succeed • Understand the culture and adapt • Strong work ethic • Be able to effectively use a computer • Remain flexible

Survey Assessment

Although industry knowledge and business expertise are beneficial, entrepreneurs need to expand their skills in order to be successful. With language as one of the greatest challenges, the entrepreneurs focused on developing their verbal and written communication skills. This provided a strong foundation on which to start their businesses. Another essential step in pursuing a venture is to understand the culture that the business is tailored to and adapting to meet the needs of the consumers. Additionally, a strong work ethic, positive attitude, and self-discipline are crucial to overcoming the challenges and tribulations that are experienced. Despite the risks, taking advantage of all the opportunities presented might help the entrepreneur change the direction or expand the business for the better. With the mindset to succeed, every entrepreneur can achieve their version of the *American Dream* and encourage others to follow in their footsteps.

Question	Responses
Lessons learned, what would be done differently?	• Plan more efficiently (have a game plan) • Save more money before investing in own business • Start the business at a younger age • Avoid partnerships and accompanying arguments • Think of the company on a larger scale • Do everything the same • Study more in school • Clocked out sooner and more often

Survey Assessment

Given the chance to start over, many entrepreneurs would make changes based on what they have experienced or learned since they began their ventures. Creating a stronger and more in-depth business plan would have helped several entrepreneurs obtain more start-up capital and open more doors in the industry. Many individuals thought additional planning, training, and classes would have increased their competitive edge and increased their customer base. Several entrepreneurs would not make any changes, believing that everything happens for a reason and that each mistake is an opportunity to learn. This contrast between making adjustments to past actions and living with no regrets creates an interesting opinion of how the previous decisions affect how we think and behave in the present and future.

Question	Responses
State of Hispanic–Latino entrepreneurship in the United States	• Differs depending on the state • High levels in coastal states • Growing stage, able to start a business anywhere • Early stages, growing as population increases • Can be difficult depending on the type of business • Open to everyone • Matured but changing

Survey Assessment

The entrepreneurs presented a large range of opinions on the state of Hispanic–Latino entrepreneurship in the United States. Several individuals believed it to be in its mature stage, reaching the peak of expansion. They viewed different markets as crowded or tapped out while others thought the level of entrepreneurship was growing at a rapid rate, especially in the coastal states. These entrepreneurs viewed different rates of expansion in different locations and in different industries. With the increase in population, more and more businesses are being developed with popular and innovative ideas to meet the growing demand. The remainder of entrepreneurs believed the Hispanic–Latino entrepreneurship to be in the beginning stages of its life cycle. The potential for success has barely been explored or realized by business owners. As more companies emerge and entrepreneurial classes become popular, individuals will become motivated to start their own businesses.

Whether in the mature, growing, or early stages of entrepreneurship, these individuals believe the market to be open to anyone and everyone who has a dream or passion to pursue their own business ventures.

Question	Responses
Membership in business organizations and its role in success	• No • Applied for Mexican Chamber of Commerce • Will look into • Restaurant organization • Professional organizations in industry • Hispanic organizations focused on leadership • InGoodCompany • Crave NYC • Pet Sitters International • National Association of Professional Pet Sitters • UNAJE (young entrepreneurs) • Applied for the New York & New Jersey Minority Supplier Development Council

Survey Assessment

The expansion of the entrepreneurial spirit has led to a variety of business organizations, offering guidance and advice to those wishing to earn a large profit and create a highly recognized brand. Many of the entrepreneurs were familiar with several organizations but were not members for a variety of reasons. Others were unaware of local or industry-related organizations but are currently looking into possible membership. Several entrepreneurs applied to a number of groups that were industry specific, age specific, and skill specific. They are hoping to obtain key business information, advice, opportunities, and a larger business network. A few entrepreneurs were active members of business organizations and saw the benefit of active participation even if the group required a fee for continued membership.

Question	Responses
Importance of social networks and networking for business success	• Built the business. • Never know who you will meet. • Delivered business cards to everyone • Attended all possible networking events • Allows for segmentation • Word of mouth • Offers free advertising • Personal connections allows for one on one interactions

Survey Assessment

Social networks and personal connections played a key role in the development of a successful business. Because networking is available to everyone, the entrepreneurs took advantage of the opportunity, reaching an expansive customer base. The often free marketing allows business owners to cultivate relationships with customers, create meaningful interactions, monitor their preferences, and create hype and excitement for their new products and services. The drawback, as seen by entrepreneurs, was the tendency of greater success and responses to come from larger businesses rather than the small start-ups. Despite the wide reach of social networking, word of mouth and personal references have proven to be a strong and reliable marketing strategy, creating repeat customers rather than one-time purchasers. No matter the medium, marketing to current and potential consumers helps create a successful and thriving business.

Questions	Responses
Advice to future generations Advice to young Hispanic–Latino entrepreneurs	• Design your path • Attend classes and workshops • Become well informed about the desired line of work • Take chances and have faith it will work out • Remain dedicated and never give up • Fight for your business • Just do it • Stay hungry and strive to be better • Be socially responsible • Be honest and kind to others • Have enough financial stability • Remain patient and soak up as much information as possible • Start now • Believe in yourself

Survey Assessment

With years of experience, the entrepreneurs had a great deal of advice for future generations of business owners. Taking active steps to become knowledgeable about the industry and developing a business plan were among the top responses. The more the entrepreneur understands about the business environment, the target market, and the specific industry, the stronger the foundation he or she has to build a strong business. Many of the entrepreneurs offered a positive mindset as a key success factor, stating that believing in oneself and viewing each setback as a learning opportunity will help to inspire the business owner to continue their venture through tough times. While some individuals thought remaining patient and soaking up as much information as possible was the way to begin the business, others believed that starting now and taking the risk will be worth the reward. Staying hungry and striving to become a stronger business helps entrepreneurs to take advantage of opportunities that could lead to a partnership, another product line, or a second storefront. The main piece of advice the entrepreneurs offered was to never give up and remain dedicated to transforming passions and dreams into reality.

Question	Responses
Participation in socio-civic organizations and philanthropic work	• No • Look forward to contributing soon • Church related activities • St. Jude hospital donation box in office • World Health Organization • Public schools • Latino classes • Promotion of healthy lifestyles • Animal Relief Fund • ASPCA • Growl Rescue • Relay for Life • Stray from the Heart • Animal Haven • Ronald McDonald House • Happy Faces Foundation

Survey Assessment

Although earning a profit and providing for their families is on the forefront of the entrepreneurs' minds, they also found it important to give back to the community and to those less fortunate. Many entrepreneurs offered financial resources to a variety of causes including healthy living, proper animal treatment, finding a cure for cancer, youth education, and families in need. In addition to monetary support, several of the entrepreneurs offered their skills, knowledge, and experience to demonstrate the importance of a strong education, living a nutritious lifestyle, and supporting causes that one is passionate about. Others offered their time to collect donations, teach children, rescue animals, speak with individuals, and share their business knowledge. Whatever the method of giving back, the entrepreneurs saw the need to help others overcome hardships, keep a positive attitude, and build a foundation for their future.

Question	Responses
Perception of business in the future and succession plans	• Business crossroads (expansion or partnership) • One person show, currently, but plan to partner with professionals • Pass the business on to another aspiring entrepreneur • Hire a team upon expansion • Son will take over the business • Owning several stores and hiring managers • Simply close down upon retirement • Keep the same values upon expansion • Pass on the business to a family member • Hiring professional managers

Survey Assessment

After thinking about how they began their businesses and the challenges they faced to become successful, the entrepreneurs looked toward the future and their succession plans. Many of the entrepreneurs were at a stage of expansion, looking toward a possible partnership or introduction of a new product or service line. In order to handle the growth of their businesses, many individuals will be hiring a team and additional managers in the near future. Several of the entrepreneurs are becoming overwhelmed by the amount of work and orders they have, which is great news but forces them to hire additional employees to take some of the stress off their backs. When the entrepreneurs retire, many hope to pass the business to a family member or child to carry on the legacy and further develop the company. Others look to hiring a professional manager to oversee the company and take the business to the next level. A few entrepreneurs were pleased with what they accomplished for their business ventures and simply desired to close down the company upon retirement.

Question	Responses
Future orientation, view of oneself 10 years onwards	• Business viewed as one of top innovative leaders • National recognition • Broadening client base • Managing own business • Buying and flipping houses • Live in the present • Expanded in central Illinois and Kentucky • Slowing down the business for retirement • Opening up more chain restaurants • Retired and living in Mexico

Survey Assessment

Looking 10 years down the road can be difficult for some entrepreneurs, especially when opportunities can appear at any time and completely alter their planned paths. Many entrepreneurs look forward to having a stronger and larger business in a decade with national brand recognition and a greater client base. Several individuals hope to expand their businesses to other regions and states, hiring more employees to handle the increase in customers. A few of the entrepreneurs are not looking far ahead but are focusing on the present and growing their business now. Some individuals aspire to become a highly successful business owner and being viewed as one of the top innovative leaders. Other than expansion and achieving accreditations, some entrepreneurs hoped to be retired and relaxing at home with their families or in another country, enjoying the fruits of their hard work and success.

Question	Responses
Legacy to the business community	• Hope to be a large factor in helping homeless pets have the opportunity to live with a family • Known for the positive impact they leave on the community • Inspire women and young children to achieve their dreams and become their own superhero • Demonstrate the possibility of growing something from nothing • Source of knowledge and advice for computer repair • Importance of being polite • Keep traditions alive • Hard worker and determined to succeed • First generation Cuban American to graduate from college • Enrich the community

Survey Assessment

With a variety of reasons the entrepreneurs began their businesses, they each desired to leave a legacy after they retired. Some individuals want to be the inspiration for other entrepreneurs, demonstrating the possibilities of never giving up, taking obstacles in stride, and pursuing opportunities they normally would not consider. Several entrepreneurs hope to be a role model for women and children to pursue their passions and become their own superheroes. While some had specific legacies, such as having a large impact in decreasing the number of homeless animals or becoming the first generation of their family to graduate from college and start a successful business, others reached toward ideals, including the importance of being honest, polite, and ethical. Particular entrepreneurs are striving to keep family and business traditions alive for future generations to learn from and expand.

Our findings point out to seven important themes in Hispanic–Latino entrepreneurship in America:

1. Real world experiences and challenges set the framework for entrepreneurial success.
2. Chronology of events and experiences triggered entrepreneurial desire and passion.
3. Hispanic–Latino entrepreneurs experienced diverse challenges but were mostly never constrained by race.
4. Family, friends, and social and professional are important for business success.
5. Hardwork, discipline, and a positive mindset are anchors for business success.
6. The state of Hispanic–Latino entrepreneurship in America is described as early, evolving, growing, and increasingly inclusive.
7. Young entrepreneurs are encouraged to start early, learn the ropes, and proactively pursue their passion.

From our study, the following may be concluded about Hispanic–Latino entrepreneurship:

1. The businesses they pursue are a result of past challenges, experiences, and learning opportunities. It may be inferred that the broader and

deeper the range of experiences the better the foundation for business success. Those interested in embarking on an entrepreneurial path are encouraged to gain theoretical as well as practical knowledge on their desired enterprises.

2. Connectivity is key. Establishing strong links with friends, family, and other networks (social and professional) tend to yield business benefits. Existing and would-be-entrepreneurs would benefit from creating a detailed plan on how to access and strengthen networks in order to derive utmost benefits.

3. There exist exciting opportunities in the future. There is substantial room for growth in the Hispanic–Latino entrepreneurial landscape. Entrepreneurs who are able to align their business passion with the right opportunity are poised to be amply rewarded.

The success of a minority group in a country is largely a result of their efforts. However, they also need to function in an environment that is supportive and embracing. The community is an important factor in supporting the business creation process (Butler and Greene 1997). Interracial harmony, socially inclusive policies, and community cooperation could stimulate faster and dynamic growth in Hispanic–Latino business.

Mentoring support can be valuable. Among Hispanics, informal mentoring has been noted as an effective methodology (Villarruel and Peragallo 2004). Mentoring is a pathway toward reaching Hispanics and contributing to their success (Guilbault and Nevaer 2012; Sotomayor 2013). Support can be found in academic institutions, church groups, professional organizations, community clubs, civic associations, chambers of commerce, friends and family, and the business community.

Finding cultural balance and suitable new roles is essential. Immigrant ethnic entrepreneurship results as an adaptive measure of an individual in response to changes in geography, culture, and psychology (Barrett, Jones, and McEvoy 1996). A well-conceived cultural transformation and evolution is necessary. For instance, among the Hispanic–Latino community, the expanding role of women is noteworthy. An A.C. Nielsen (2013) report pointed out that (1) Latinas are well educated, technologically adept, and socially connected; (2) About 86 percent of Latin women take an active role in the purchasing decisions in their households; and (3) Latinas take dominant roles in purchases of goods such as food, beverages, clothes, and pharmaceuticals. Along with the men, Latin women will play a significant role in the future of entrepreneurship in the country.

Maintaining cultural identity and spirituality are important future anchors. Some cultural norms and practices are slowly eroding. For instance, the number of Hispanic Catholics is declining, with about 24 percent of Hispanic adults described as former Catholics (Pew Research 2014). Similar to young American adults, Hispanic Millennials have lower rates of religious affiliation and commitment than their older counterparts (Martinez and Lipka 2014). Regardless of one's religiosity and preference, cultural and spiritual identities serve as a moral compass that directs one's personal and business growth.

Having the courage and perseverance to overcome obstacles in life and business is paramount. Immigrant entrepreneurs need to overcome "blocked opportunities" (Barrett, Jones, and McEvoy 1996). Education, capital, and previous experience, as well as parents' work, have been deemed important to business success (Marger 1989). If these factors become barriers to business formation or growth, Hispanic–Latino entrepreneurs need to dig deep and work through the challenges in order to achieve their goals. In the words of Victor Rodriguez, President of LatAm Alternatives, a Florida-based financial services company, "I came to this country with no English, no money, and no network, but I was ready for the American dream." (Scotti 2012).

Bouchikhi (1993) postulated that successful entrepreneurship requires dealing with chaos and complexity, and necessitates a viable linkage between factors such as entrepreneurial personality and behavior, environment, and chance in order to have a favorable outcome. In the case of Hispanic–Latino entrepreneurs, the findings indicate that the right combination of personality and behavior, the environment in which the business operated, and the timing when the opportunity presented itself, led to business success.

Minority entrepreneurs looking to start a business in a foreign country do not face an easy task. Challenges relating to social issues, language, education barriers, and the inability to access capital can serve as obstacles. Nevertheless, as our interviewees demonstrated, there is a way to overcome these challenges.

There is a huge window of opportunity for minority entrepreneurs, such as Hispanics and Latinos to not only survive in business, but win in a big way. The factors that lead to success is not solely anchored on capital, education, or even role models. The primary determinant for entrepreneurial success among Hispanic Latinos is self-motivation and the will power to convert a dream into reality. In essence, it's about knowing oneself and having the vision, commitment, and drive to make things happen.

About the Authors

Dr. J. Mark Munoz is a professor of international business at Millikin University, Illinois, and a former visiting fellow at the Kennedy School of Government at Harvard University. He is a recipient of several awards including three Best Research Paper Awards, Teaching Excellence Awards, and a literary award. In 2012, he was honored as the 2012 Distinguished Scholar by the Academy of Global Business Advancement. In 2013, he received a teaching excellence award from the Accreditation Council for Business Schools and Programs (ACBSP). Aside from top-tier journal publications, he has authored, coauthored, and edited eight books, namely: *Land of My Birth*, *Winning Across Borders*, *In Transition*, *A Salesman in Asia*, *Handbook of Business Plan Creation*, *International Social Entrepreneurship*, *Contemporary Microenterprises: Concepts and Cases*, and *Handbook on the Geopolitics of Business*. In 2014, he was admitted as Fellow to the Royal Geographical Society.

Dr. Michelle Ingram Spain is the Director of the Deville School of Business Center for Business Collaboration and Associate Professor at the Walsh University Deville School of Business, North Canton, Ohio.

Her publications include a chapter in *Contemporary Microenterprise*, Edgar Publishing 2010; and some of her forthcoming works include: *African American Entrepreneurship: Profiles and Viewpoints* scheduled for publication in 2015, *Hispanic–Latino Entrepreneurship: Profile and Viewpoints* scheduled for publication 2014. Her recent presentations include publication of a Microenterprise Development Model for Training Developmentally and Physically Challenged Individuals (Dreams Lived, Not Deferred and Minority Entrepreneurial Mindset). She is the coach and faculty advisor for the Walsh University Collegiate Entrepreneurship Organization Chapter and has mentored participants in the invitations only Texas Christian University (TCU) Venture and Values Business Plan Competition. She is a certified small business counselor and small business loan intermediary, was the former director of the David Myers University Minority Small Business Assistance Center and Small Business Development undergraduate program.

Dr. Spain was an assistant professor and coordinator of the Organizational Behavior Program at Case Western Reserve University, Cleveland, Ohio, where she founded and directed the region 8 Ohio Minority Business Assistance Center, Ohio Ward 2 Entrepreneur Scholars Program, the Cuyahoga County Board of Mental Retardation and Development Entrepreneurial Training and Development Program, as well as the Satellite Miles Health Center Small Business Assistance Collaboration.

Dr. Spain currently serves on numerous social enterprise organizations and small business development and civic engagement organizations advisory boards.

Dr. Spain is the recipient of the SBA Regional Minority Small Business Advocate Award, the Small Business Provider Award, the Cleveland Rotary Paul Harris Fellow for the Development and implementation of the award winning Cleveland Rotary Small Business Mentor Protégé Program, the Communication Association Rock and Roll City Program Diversity Award, Who's Who Cleveland, and Crain's Business Daily 40 Most Influential Women ABC Heroes and Heroines. She received her doctorate degree from Teacher's College, Columbia University.

References

A.C. Nielsen. 2013. "Latinas Are a Driving Force behind Hispanic Purchasing Power." *Newswire.* http://www.nielsen.com/us/en/newswire/2013/latinas-are-a-driving-force-behind-hispanic-purchasing-power-in-.html, (accessed on May 29, 2014).

Barrett, G.A., T.P. Jones, and D. McEvoy. 1996. "Ethnic Minority Business: Theoretical Discourse in Britain and North America." *Urban Studies* 33, no. 4–5, pp. 783–809.

Barth, J., G. Yago, and B. Zeidman. 2006. "Barriers to Entrepreneurship in Emerging Domestic Markets: Analysis and Recommendations." Working Paper, Milken Institute. www.utahlifescience.com/econ_dev_reports/Milken_Barriers_Entrepreneurship.pdf, (accessed on July 12, 2012).

Bates, T.M. 1997. *Race, Self-employment and Upward Mobility: An Illusive American Dream.* Washington, DC: The Woodrow Wilson Center Press.

Boden, R.J., and B. Headd. 2002. "Race and Gender Differences in Business Ownership and Business Turnover: An Empirical Study Using a New, Unique Data Series." *Business Economics* 37, no. 4, pp. 61–72.

Borjas, G.J. 1986. "The Self-employment Experience of Immigrants." *The Journal of Human Resources* 21, no. 4, pp. 485–506.

Bouchikhi, H. 1993. "A Constructivist Framework for Understanding Entrepreneurship Performance." *Organization Studies* 14, no. 4, pp. 549–570.

Butler, J.S., and P.G. Greene. 1997. "Ethnic Entrepreneurship: The Continuous Rebirth of American Entrepreneurship." In *Entrepreneurship 2000*, eds. D.L. Sexton and R.W. Smilor, 267–289. Chicago, IL: Upstart Publishing,

Cardon, M.S., R.S. Shinnar, M. Eisenman, and E.G. Rogoff. 2008. "Segmenting the Population of Entrepreneurs: A Cluster Study Analysis." *Journal of Developmental Entrepreneurship* 13, no. 3, pp. 293–314.

Carvajal, M. 2004. "Measuring Economic Discrimination of Hispanic-Owned Architecture and Engineering Firms in South Florida." *Hispanic Journal of Behavioral Sciences* 26, pp. 79–101.

Clark, M.A., S. Lee, W. Goodman, and S. Yacco. 2008. "Examining Male Underachievement in Public Education: Action Research at a District Level." *NASSP Bulletin* 92, no. 2, pp. 111–132.

Crook, J. 1996. "Credit Constraints and US Households." *Applied Financial Economics* 6, no. 6, pp. 477–485.

Cummings, S., ed. 1980. *Self-help in Urban America: Patterns of Minority Business Enterprise*. London: Kennikat Press.

Dadzie, K., and Y. Cho. 1989. "Determinants of Minority Business Formation and Survival: An Empirical Assessment." *Journal of Small Business Management* 27, pp. 56–61.

De Freitas, G. 1991. *Inequality at Work: Hispanics in the U.S. Labor Force*. New York: Oxford University Press.

Enz, CA, M.J. Dollinger, and C.M. Daily. 1990. "The Value Orientations of Minority and Non-minority Small Business Owners." *Entrepreneurship Theory and Practice* 15, no. 1, pp. 23–35.

Fairlie, R.W. 2008. Estimating the Contribution of Immigrant Business Owners to the U.S. Economy. Working Paper at SBA Office of Advocacy.

Fairlie, R.W., and A. Robb. 2007. "Families, Human Capital, and Small Business: Evidence from the Characteristics of Business Owners Survey." *Industrial and Labor Relations Review* 60, no. 2, pp. 225–245.

Fairlie, R.W., and C. Woodruff. 2006. *Mexican-American Entrepreneurship*. http://people.ucsc.edu/~rfairlie/papers/published/bejournals%202010%20-%20mexican%20american%20entrepreneurship.pdf (accessed on Oct 24, 2014).

Feldman, H.D., C.S. Koberg, and T.J. Dean. 1991. "Minority Small Business Owners and Their Paths to Ownership." *Journal of Small Business Management* 29, no. 4, pp. 12–28.

Fox, E.J. 2014. "Number of U.S. Millionaires Hits New High." *Economy*, CNN Money. http://money.cnn.com/2014/03/14/news/economy/us-million-aires-households/, (accessed on June 4, 2014).

Fratoe, F.A. 1986. "A Sociological Analysis of Minority Business." *The Review of Black Political Economy* 15, no. 2, pp. 5–29.

Gavino, M., and R. Ortiz-Walters. 2011. "Use of Business Resources by Latino and Latina Entrepreneurs: Toward a Better Understanding of this Under-Utilization Dilemma." *Business Journal of Hispanic Research* 5, no. 1, pp. 16–30.

Guilbault, R.C., and L.E.V. Nevaer. 2012. *The Latino's Guide to Success in the Workplace*. Santa Barbara, CA: ABC-CLIO.

Harris, J., R. Saltstone, and M. Fraboni. 1999. "An Evaluation of the Job Stress Questionnaire with a Sample of Entrepreneurs." *Journal of Business and Psychology* 13, no. 3, pp. 447–455.

Harwood, E. 1982. "The Sociology of Entrepreneurship." In *Encyclopedia of Entrepreneurship*, eds. C. Kent, D. Sexton, and K. Vesper, 92–98. Englewood Cliffs, NJ: Prentice Hall.

Jennings, J.E., and M.S. McDougald. 2007. "Work-Family Interface Experiences and Coping Strategies: Implications for Entrepreneurship Research and Practice." *Academy of Management Review* 32, no. 3, pp. 747–757.

Jones, J.M. 2013. "U.S. Blacks, Hispanics Have No Preference on Group Label," *Gallup Politics.* http://www.gallup.com/poll/163706/blacks-hispanics-no-preferences-group-labels.aspx, (accessed on May 29, 2014).

Jones, K. 1995. "An Investigation of the Psychodynamics Associated with Ethnic Entrepreneurship." *Academy of Entrepreneurship Journal* 1, no. 1, pp. 53–64.

Kamo, Y. 2000. "Racial and Ethnic Differences in Extended Family Households." *Sociological Perspectives* 43, no. 2, pp. 211–229.

Kirchhoff, B.A., R.L. Stevens, and N.I. Hurwitz (1982). "Factors Underlying Increases in Minority Entrepreneurship 1972–1977." In *Frontiers of Entrepreneurship Research*, ed. K.H. Vesper. Wellesley, MA: Babson College Center for Entrepreneurial Studies.

Kochhar, R., C.S. Espinoza, and R. Hinze-Pifer. 2010. *After the Great Recession: Foreign-Born Gain Jobs: Native Born Lose Jobs.* Washington, DC: Pew Hispanic Center.

Krogstad, J.M., and M.H. Lopez. 2014. "Hispanic Nativity Shift: U.S. Births Drive Population Growth as Immigration Stalls." *Pew Research: Hispanic Trends Project.* http://www.pewhispanic.org/2014/04/29/hispanic-nativity-shift/, (accessed on May 29, 2014).

Lee, Y., T. Cameroen, P. Schaeffer, and C.G. Schmidt. 1997. "Ethnic Minority Small Business: A Comparative Analysis of Restaurants in Denver." *Urban Geography* 18, no. 7, pp. 591–621.

Lichtenstein, G., and T.S. Lyons. 1996. *Incubating New Enterprises.* Washington, DC: Aspen Institute.

Light, I. 1979. "Disadvantaged Minorities in Self-employment." *International Journal of Comparative Sociology* 20, no. 1–2, pp. 31–45.

Light, I., and C. Rosenstein. 1995. *Race, Ethnicity and Entrepreneurship in Urban America.* New York: Aldine Grayton.

Light, I, G. Sabagh, M. Bozorgmehr, and C. Der-Martirosian. 1994. "Beyond the Ethnic Enclave Economy." *Social Problems* 41, no. 1, pp. 65–80.

Lofstrom, M., and C. Wang. 2006. "Hispanic Self-employment: A Dynamic Analysis of Business Ownership." Working Paper IZA DP 2101, Institute for the Study of Labor. http://www.econstor.eu/bitstream/10419/33581/1/511408447.pdf

Lowrey, Y. 2004. "Dynamics of Minority-Owned Employer Establishments 1997–2001." Research Paper, U.S. Small Business Administration, Office of Advocacy.

Lynch, E.W., and M.J. Hanson, eds. 2004. *Developing Cross-Cultural Competence: A Guide for Working with Children and Their Families.* Baltimore, MD: Paul H. Brookes.

Marger, M. 1989. "Business Strategies among East-Indian Entrepreneurs in Toronto: The Role of Group Resources and Opportunity Structure." *Ethnic and Racial Studies* 12, no. 4, pp. 539–563.

Martinez, J., and M. Lipka. 2014. "Hispanic Millennials Are Less Religious Than Older U.S. Hispanics." *Fact Tank*, Pew Research Center. http://www.pewresearch.org/fact-tank/2014/05/08/hispanic-millennials-are-less-religious-than-older-u-s-hispanics/, (accessed on May 29, 2014).

Mora, M.T., and A. Dávila. 2006. "Mexican Immigrants Self-Employment along the US–Mexico Border: An Analysis of 2000 Census Data." *Social Science Quarterly* 87, no. 1, pp. 91–109.

Munnell, A.H., L.E. Browne, J. McEneaney, and G.M.B. Tootell. 1996. "Mortgage Lending in Boston: Interpreting HMDA Data." *American Economic Review* 86, 1, pp. 25–53.

Orrenius, P.M., and M. Zavodny. 2009. "Tied to the Business Cycle: How Immigrants Fare in Good and Bad Economic Times." *Migration Policy Institute*, pp. 1–37.

Pew Research. 2013. "2011 Hispanic Origin Profiles." *Hispanic Trends Project, Pew Research.* http://www.pewhispanic.org/2013/06/19/hispanic-origin-profiles/, (accessed on May 29, 2013).

Pew Research. 2014. "The Shifting Religious Identity of Latinos in the United States." *Religion and Public Life Project, Pew Research.* http://www.pewforum.org/2014/05/07/the-shifting-religious-identity-of-latinos-in-the-united-states/, (accessed on May 29, 2014).

Porter, C. 2011. "Hispanics are Largest Minority Group in US." IIP Digital. http://iipdigital.usembassy.gov/st/english/article/2011/03/20110328152807enelrahc0.5275232.html#axzz3DfDrmmTa, (accessed on July 13, 2012).

Ragins, B.R., and K.E. Kram. 2007. *The Handbook of Mentoring at Work.* Los Angeles, CA: Sage.

Raijman, R. 2001. "Mexican Immigrants and Informal Self-employment: A Case Study in the City of Chicago." *Human Organization* 60, no. 1, pp. 47–55.

Raijman, R., and M. Tienda. 2000. "Immigrants' Pathways to Business Ownership: A Comparative Ethnic Perspective." *International Migration Review* 34, no. 3, pp. 681–705.

Rivera, A., B. Cotto-Escalera, A. Desai, J. Huezo, and D. Muhammad. 2008. *Foreclosed: State of the Dream.* Boston, MA: United for a Fair Economy.

Robb, A.M. 2002. "Entrepreneurial Performance by Women and Minorities: The Case of New Firms." *Journal of Developmental Entrepreneurship* 7, no. 4, pp. 383–397.

Rogers, C.D., M.J. Gent, G.M. Palumbo, and R.A. Wall. 2001. "Understanding the Growth and Viability of Inner City Businesses." *Journal of Developmental Entrepreneurship* 6, no. 3, pp. 237–254.

Saenz, V., and L. Ponjuan. 2009. "The Vanishing Latino Male in Higher Education." *Journal of Hispanic Higher Education* 8, no. 1, pp. 54–89.

Scott, W.L. 1983. "Financial Performance on Minority versus Non-Minority-Owned Businesses." *Journal of Small Business Management* 21, no. 1, pp. 42–48.

Scotti, M. June 2012. "Made in America." *Traders Magazine*, pp. 48–52.

Shim, S., and M.A. Eastlick. 1998. "Characteristics of Hispanic Female Business Owners: An Exploratory Study." *Journal of Small Business Management* 36, no. 3, pp. 18–34.

SBA (Small Business Administration). 2005. The Small Business Economy for Data Year 2005: A Report to the President. www.sba.gov/advo/research/sb_econ2006.pdf

Smith-Hunter, A.E. 2006. "An Initial Look at the Characteristics of Hispanic Women Business Owners and Their Businesses." *Business Renaissance Quarterly* 1, no. 2, pp. 101–140.

Snyder, T.D., and S.A. Dillow. 2011. *Digest of Education Statistics 2010*. Washington, DC: National Center for Education Statistics.

Sotomayor, S.M. 2013. *My Beloved World.* New York: Knopf.

Stone, D.L., R.D. Johnson, E.F. Stone-Romero, and M. Hartman. 2006. "A Comparative Study of Hispanic-American and Anglo-American Cultural Values and Job Choice Preferences." *Management Research* 4, pp. 8–21.

Taylor, P., M.H. Lopez, J. Martinez, and G. Velasco. 2012. "When Labels Don't Fit: Hispanics and Their View of Identity," *Hispanic Trends Project, Pew Research.* http://www.pewhispanic.org/2012/04/04/when-labels-dont-fit-hispanics-and-their-views-of-identity/, (accessed on May 29, 2014).

Telles, E.E., and V. Ortiz. 2008. *Generations of Exclusion: Mexican Americans, Assimilation, and Race.* New York: Russell Sage Foundation.

Tienda, M., and R. Raijman. 2004. "Promoting Hispanic Entrepreneurship in Chicago." *Journal of Developmental Entrepreneurship* 9, no. 1, pp. 1–21.

U.S. Census Bureau. 2006. "U.S. Hispanic Population: 2006." http://www.census.gov/population/socdemo/hispanic/cps2006/CPS_Powerpoint_2006.pdf, (accessed on May 30, 2008).

U.S. Census Bureau. 2007. "American Fact Finder." www.factfinder.census.gov, (accessed on July 12, 2012).

U.S. Census Bureau. "Census Bureau Reports Hispanic-Owned Businesses Increase at More Than Double the National Rate." http://www.census.gov/newsroom/releases/archives/business_ownership/cb10-145.html, (accessed on July 13, 2013).

U.S. Census Bureau. 2012. "Statistics about Business Size (Including Small Business) from the U.S. Census Bureau." www.census.gov/epcd/www/smallbus.html

Villareal, R., and R.A. Peterson. 2008. "Hispanic Ethnicity and Media Behavior." *Journal of Advertising Research* 48, no. 2, pp. 179–190.

Villarruel, A.M., and N. Peragallo. 2004. "Leadership Development of Hispanic Nurses." *Nursing Administration Quarterly* 28, no. 3, pp. 173–180.

Vincent, V. 1996. "Decision-Making Policies among Mexican American Small Business Entrepreneurs." *Journal of Small Business Management* 34, no. 4, pp. 1–13.

Webber, R.A. 1969. *Culture and Management: Text and Readings in Comparative Management.* Homewood, IL: Richard D. Irwin Inc.

Wolfe, L. 2012. "Which is Politically Correct: Latino or Hispanic?" Women in Business. http://womeninbusiness.about.com/od/businessetiquette/a/pc-hispanic.htm, (accessed on July 13, 2012).

Index

www.ingramcontent.com/pod-product-compliance
Lightning Source LLC
Chambersburg PA
CBHW062013200326

41519CB00017B/4792